BEIJING

Edited by Don J Cohn

GW00493479

Hong Kong

© 1992, 1988 The Guidebook Company Ltd

All rights reserved.

Grateful acknowledgment is made to the following authors and publishers for permissions granted:

University of Hawaii Press for
The Venerable Schoolmaster Gao, by Lu Xun, translated by William A Lyell,
© 1990 University of Hawaii

and

Rickshaw by Lao She, translated by Jean M James, © 1979 The University Press of Hawaii

Cambridge University Press for
The Travels and Controversies of Friar Domingo Navarrete 1618–1686,
edited by J S Cummins, © 1962 The Hakluyt Society

George Allen & Unwin,
now Unwin Hyman of HarperCollins Publishers Limited for
Arthur Waley Chinese Poems Copyright year 1946,

George N Kates for
The Years That Were Fat by George N Kates, © 1966 George N Kates

From the *City of Lingering Splendour* by John Blofeld. © 1961 by John Blofeld. Reprinted by
arrangement with Shambhala Publications Inc, 300 Massachusetts Ave, Boston MA 02115

Chatto & Windus Publishers and Peters Fraser & Dunlop for
The Gunpowder Gardens by Jason Goodwin. © 1990 Jason Goodwin

Random Century Group and Jonathan Cape Ltd for
Destination Chungking by Han Suyin

Distribution in the United Kingdom, Ireland, Europe and certain Commonwealth countrie by Hodder
& Stoughton, Mill Road, Dunton Green, Sevenoaks, Kent TN13 2YA

Editor: Don J Cohn
Series Editor: Claire Banham
Illustrations Editor: Caroline Robertson
Map Artwork: Bai Yiliang
Cover Concept: Raquel Jaramillo and Aubrey Tse
Design: U Wang Graphics
Production House: Twin Age Limited, Hong Kong
Printed by Sing Cheong Printing Company Limited, Hong Kong
Photography: Front cover by Steve Vidler, Stockhouse; back cover by Richard Dobson;
Basil Pao 158, 159; Magnus Bartlett 5, 8, 13, 75, 82, 95, 110, 138, 139, 143, 184, 189; Don J
Cohn 48, 78–79; Hanart T Z Gallery 25, 142; Hongkong and Shanghai Bank Group Archives
55, 155; Ingrid Morejohn 62; James Montogomery 128; John Warner Publications 22–23, 69;
Richard Dobson 9, 16, 30, 31, 34–35, 39, 51, 102, 124, 161, 168, 172, 177, 203; The Commer-
cial Press Ltd 63, 89, 107, 201; courtesy of the Board of Trustees of the Victoria and Albert
Museum, London 134, 165; Wattis Fine Art 71, 90–91, 150

Contents

Maps

Special Topics

Excerpts

Introduction
by Don J Cohn

At no time since Marco Polo wrote his *Travels* in the 13th century has the grand old city of Beijing received so much publicity as during the summer of 1989.

Throughout April and May that year, millions around the globe stayed glued to their televisions as the vast central square in the capital of the world's most populous nation filled with Chinese students and other citizens in what was undoubtedly the largest spontaneous public gathering in China since the founding of the People's Republic. Soviet President Mikhail Gorbachev was in Beijing meeting with China's elder statesman, Deng Xiaoping. But the Chinese people had first come to the Square to mourn the death, on 15 April, of deposed Communist Party Secretary Hu Yaobang, and to petition the government for a reevaluation of his role in Party history. As spring moved into summer, the crowds in the Square swelled, and the general mood swiftly changed from lamentation to protest. Martial law was declared in the Square in late May, but it had little effect on the crowds, who had set up camps there and were determined to stay until the government agreed to engage in a dialogue on such issues as corruption, nepotism and inflation (the latter had reached a record post-1949 level of 30 percent). A televised meeting took place between state leaders and representatives of the demonstrators, but this did little to dispel the growing tension. Tanks and armed personnel carriers of the People's Liberation Army had been moving towards the centre of the city for a number of days. And then, in the early hours of 4 June, following the issuance of a government warning, troops entered the square in an action officially referred to as 'the suppression of the counter-revolutionary insurrection'. The actual number of people killed as a result is still in dispute but there is no doubt about the enormity of the tragedy.

The events in Tiananmen had a chilling effect on the flow of diplomatic kindness from the West to China, particularly after machine-gun bullets penetrated the walls of buildings occupied by foreign diplomats and businessmen. But most Western governments found it expedient to overlook the damage the crackdown had caused, and by late 1991 China had regained most of the diplomatic ground it had lost since 1989.

As one might expect, foreign tourism in China declined sharply in the aftermath. However, the spring of 1990 saw the beginning of a recovery that has continued through 1991, with Overseas Chinese, 'Taiwanese compatriots', and China's other Asian neighbours making up the bulk of the visitors. In Beijing alone, there are now over 200 hotels that accept foreign guests, compared to fewer than ten in 1978. Many of these properties had come on stream in 1989 and 1990, creating a serious room glut, particularly in Beijing, Shanghai and Xi'an, with nearly every hotel reporting low occupancy rates and offering sharp discounts. The scars of 4 June are healing slowly, aided by short-term memories. China may no longer be chic, but perhaps people understand her better.

Examining the role that Beijing plays in the Chinese scheme of things may shed some light on why the authorities felt it necessary to suppress the 'turmoil' in Tiananmen Square in such a decisive way, and why at the same time the city casts such an ineluctable spell on visitors from afar.

Beijing is the source of all authority in China, the political, military, economic and cultural centre of the country. It is home to China's top power brokers and vast central bureaucracy, to legions of veteran revolutionaries, state-sponsored artists and writers, and a wide spectrum of international friends, as well as to diplomats and businessmen from more than 100 countries. While China is formally a proletarian dictatorship, political scientists estimate that the country is run in practice by about 150 men and a few women, all of them based in the capital. Beijng is also headquarters for the 14 venerable revolutionary families whose scions control much of the lucrative international trade in strategic commodities and manufactured goods.

After ten years of practising 'socialism with Chinese characteristics', China can now boast income differentials comparable to those of Hong Kong. For every rag and bone picker—recycling engineers at the grass roots level—who sleeps in an adobe *hutong* hut, there is now at least one renminbi millionaire (US$187,266 at the official rate) driving around in an imported car and ordering Peking duck over a portable telephone. Deng Xiaoping's policy of opening to the outside world and relaxing the centre's rigid grip on the domestic economy was a categorical rejection of most of what the Cultural Revolution stood for, in that it contributed to a sharp rise in the quantity and quality of material benefits available to the average citizen, albeit with gross inequalities of distribution.

How far can economic progress go without political change? China has been ruled from inside a single set of walls for too long. The *glasnost* sought by the crowds in Tiananmen Square will only become a reality once this tradition evolves to confront the realities of the 21st century. But no one on either side of the walls knows how to proceed.

The present sanctum sanctorum of state power is located in Zhongnanhai, a Chinese Emerald City set in a former imperial garden on the shores of a man-made lake created in the Ming Dynasty, and surrounded by the tallest extant walls in the city. Mao Zedong personally selected Zhongnanhai in the late 1940s to serve as the citadel of the Chinese Communist Party after rejecting the Forbidden City for security reasons.

Zhongnanhai had been the site of the presidential mansion during the early years of the short-lived Republic of China (1911–1949), and before that it was the Western Garden of the Ming and Qing emperors. Chairman Mao fortified the former pleasure grounds, transforming it into a top-security bastion with an underground military command centre, fall-out shelters, helicopter pad and secret tunnels leading to the Great Hall of the People and military airport in the western suburbs. It was from Zhongnanhai that Mao ruled China for 27 years.

But this intimidating collage is just one aspect of the city. On the other, more crowded side of the tracks, the lot of the average Beijing citizen differs little from that of city folk elsewhere in China. A striking emergence (or resurfacing) of middle class values and pursuits has taken place in every urban centre in the country over the last decade. In Beijing and elsewhere, the shops are filled with a wide and familiar range of consumer goods, there seems to be no lack of restaurants or food to eat, and there are many new and revived traditional ways—both legal and illegal— for people to spend their leisure time and surplus cash. Many of the bustling Chinese you will encounter at the major tourist spots, such as the Great Wall, Forbidden City, Chairman Mao's mausoleum, Summer Palace and Temple of Heaven, are tourists from out of town, as their accents and sometimes their dress reveals. You are more likely to encounter Beijing residents in parks in the early morning, when they congregate in the fresh air to practice *taiji*, *wushu* (martial arts) or *qigong* breath energy excercises, often with a fervour that approaches religious devotion. Or you may observe them haggling over the price of a chicken or expertly fingering a watermelon in a free market.

Since 1978, Chinese society has waxed materialistic and consumerist, and in most Chinese cities, Beijing in particular, money buys nearly everything, although for that stretch Mercedes you probably have to go through the back door, or depend on special *guanxi* or personal connections. If you smoke, for instance, imported cigarettes, many of them smuggled into China via the Guangdong coast from Hong Kong, are sold on street corners for soft currency. If you want to get weighed, next to the cigarette pedlar sits Grandma Wang, who runs a weighing service using her bathroom scales. Five *fen* a shot, or less than one US cent.

For the foreign visitor, who may have come to China to escape the pressures of the materialistic world, the spiritual and aesthetic delights of Beijing are numerous: pottering about the unfrequented corners of imperial palaces and gardens; getting lost in the medieval maze of *hutongs*, lanes and alleys; listening to amateur singers crooning Peking opera on a warm summer night in a willow-shaded park; sharing a table and a bottle of 'white lightning' clear spirits with the locals at a noisy crowded restaurant.

Like a rural village, Beijing comes alive at sunrise. Street sweepers begin their rounds at 5 am, and the joggers and exercisers are in their places by 6 am. Commuting begins well before 7 am as most people begin working at 8 am. By 10 am the food markets are crowded with housewives buying their pork and peppers for lunch. From about noon to 2 pm, all of Beijing seems to hibernate. The groggy afternoon ends around 4 pm when the evening rush hour begins. Dinner is served at 6 pm, the TV is switched on for the evening news at 7 pm, and by 10 pm most of Beijing is ready for bed. Now do the honey pots from the suburban farms, pulled by horses and donkeys and manned by stoical peasants, make the rounds of the city's latrines collecting the enriched urban night soil.

The first-time visitor to Beijing is likely to be overwhelmed by the seemingly endless tidal flow of cyclists during rush hour; by the size of the monuments and vastness of the public spaces; by the third-world sanitary conditions; and by the odd contradictions inherent in ancient cities that can be felt but not seen. Beijing shares most of the everyday problems faced by major metropolises worldwide, with the exception of widespread street crime, but this is compensated for by a unique architectural heritage, quality hotels and restaurants, and some splendid museums and sights.

To get a feel for the city, take any public bus to the end of the line and back. It may be impossible to get a seat, not to mention a few square centimetres of floor space of your own, but this is an ideal opportunity for people-watching. You will learn about local geography, and be massaged into the relaxed pace at which much of the city moves. Browse in the bookstores, the food markets and the antiques shops. Take a pedicab from Qianmen to Liulichang, but only after haggling over the price. Spend an hour in the warm atmosphere of a bathhouse, if you don't mind curious stares. Try to identify the ineffable local dialect, *Beijing hua*, with its drawled 'r' at the ends of words. To the uninitiated, speakers of *Beijing hua* always seem to be on the verge of swallowing their tongues. Somehow it sounds distinctly Texan. Wander around Tiananmen Square when no one is there but the spirits. Watch the sun rise over the blue-tiled roofs of the Temple of Heaven and set over the Western (Fragrant) Hills from the shores of Kunming Lake in the Summer Palace. Linger long enough in the Palace for the tourist hordes to file out (around 4 pm) and share something of the imperial solitude and isolation experienced by the emperors and their ladies.

In a great walled civilisation like China, the more you know about what happens on the inside the better. Read something of the history of the Ming and Qing dynasties, much of which was played out in the places you will visit. Or immerse yourself in Pekingiana, that vast corpus of books written about the city by Chinese and foreign travellers, journalists, poets and pilgrims, excerpts of which are interspersed throughout this guidebook. Read about Marco Polo who, incidentally, like many other 'China experts' may never have been to Beijing or only passed through the capital on a brief tour. Many of Marco's records tally with the Chinese history books, but he was never mentioned in them.

And what of the legacy of the past? By any sober assessment, Old Peking was dead and buried by the mid-20th century and no one can doubt that New Beijing is here to stay. But in China, perhaps more than elsewhere, the past lingers on, patiently defying the present before swallowing it up.

Yet Old Peking is elusive—the refined manners, customs and material culture of a vanishing world, flickerings of which survive in long-time residents in their seventies, eighties and beyond. History has imposed a gentle discipline on the members of this generation, a discipline that young people, raised on revolution and rising expectations, naturally find unacceptable. Many young Chinese are now looking to the West for the solution to the problems China is

Summer Palace 頤和園.

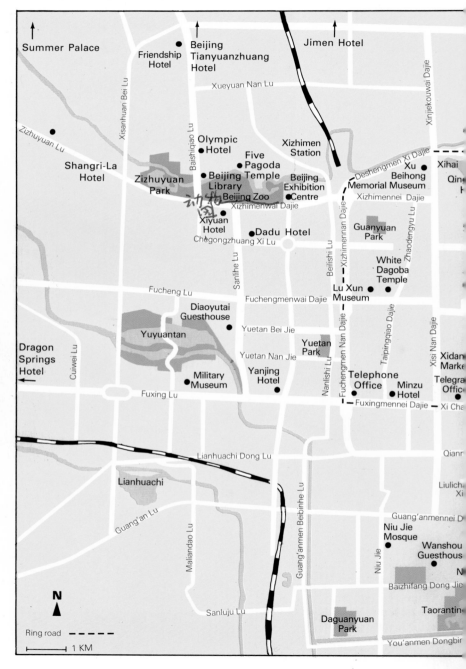

Summer Palace

Friendship Hotel

Beijing Tianyuanzhuang Hotel

Jimen Hotel

Xueyuan Nan Lu

Xisanhuan Bei Lu

Baishiqiao Lu

Xinjiekouwai Dajie

Zizhuyuan Lu

Shangri-La Hotel

Zizhuyuan Park

Olympic Hotel

Five Pagoda Temple

Beijing Library

Beijing Zoo

动物园

Xizhimen Station

Beijing Exhibition Centre

Deshengmen Xi Dajie

Xu Beihong Memorial Museum

Xihai

Qin H

Xizhimennei Dajie

Xizhimenwai Dajie

Zhaodengyu Lu

Xiyuan Hotel

Dadu Hotel

Chegongzhuang Xi Lu

Guanyuan Park

Beilishi Lu

Xizhimennan Dajie

White Dagoba Temple

Santihe Lu

Fucheng Lu

Fuchengmenwai Dajie

Lu Xun Museum

Diaoyutai Guesthouse

Yuyuantan

Yuetan Bei Jie

Fuchengmen Nan Dajie

Taipingqiao Dajie

Xisi Nan Dajie

Cuiwei Lu

Yuetan Nan Jie

Yuetan Park

Nanlishi Lu

Xidan Market

Dragon Springs Hotel

Military Museum

Yanjing Hotel

Telephone Office

Minzu Hotel

Telegra Offic

Fuxing Lu

Fuxingmennei Dajie

Xi Cha

Lianhuachi Dong Lu

Qianr

Lianhuachi

Guang'an Lu

Maliandao Lu

Guang'anmen Beibinhe Lu

Guang'anmennei D

Liulicha Xi

Niu Jie Mosque

Wanshou Guesthous

Niu Jie

N

Baizhifang Dong Jie

Ring road - - - -

1 KM

Sanluju Lu

Daguanyuan Park

Taorantin

You'anmen Dongbir

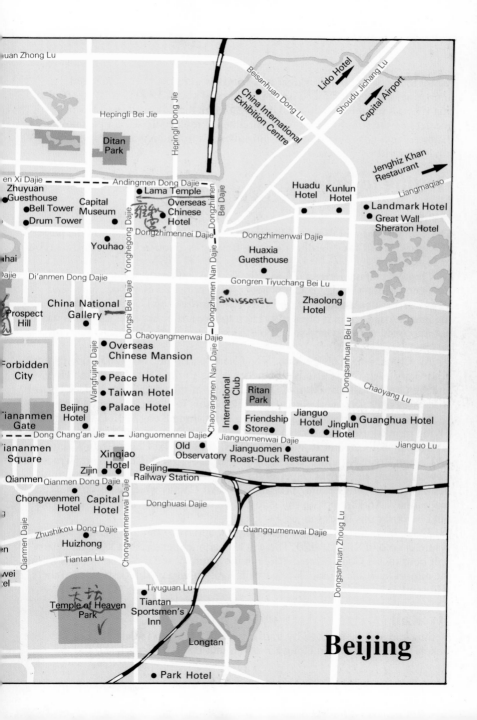

Huan Zhong Lu

Beisanhuan Dong Lu

Lido Hotel

Shoudu Jichang Lu

Capital Airport

China International Exhibition Centre

Hepingli Bei Jie

Hepingli Dong Jie

Ditan Park

Jenghiz Khan Restaurant

Liangmaqiao

en Xi Dajie — — — Andingmen Dong Dajie — —

Zhuyuan Guesthouse

Bell Tower

Drum Tower

Capital Museum

Lama Temple

雍和宫

Overseas Chinese Hotel

Huadu Hotel

Kunlun Hotel

Landmark Hotel

Great Wall Sheraton Hotel

Yonghegong Dajie

Dongzhimennei Dajie

Dongzhimen Bei Dajie

Dongzhimenwai Dajie

Youhao

hai

Dajie

Di'anmen Dong Dajie

Dongsi Bei Dajie

Huaxia Guesthouse

Dongzhimen Nan Dajie

Gongren Tiyuchang Bei Lu

SWISSOTEL

Zhaolong Hotel

Dongsanhuan Bei Lu

Chaoyang Lu

China National Gallery

Prospect Hill

Chaoyangmenwai Dajie

Wangfujing Dajie

Overseas Chinese Mansion

Chaoyangmen Nan Dajie

Forbidden City

Peace Hotel

Taiwan Hotel

Palace Hotel

International Club

Ritan Park

Jianguo Hotel

Guanghua Hotel

Beijing Hotel

Friendship Store

Jinglun Hotel

Tiananmen Gate

— Dong Chang'an Jie — — Jianguomennei Dajie

Jianguomenwai Dajie

Jianguo Lu

Tiananmen Square

Xinqiao Hotel

Zijin

Old Observatory

Jianguomen Roast-Duck Restaurant

Qianmen

Qianmen Dong Dajie

Chongwenmenwai Dajie

Beijing Railway Station

Chongwenmen Hotel

Capital Hotel

Donghuasi Dajie

Guangqumenwai Dajie

Dongsanhuan Zhoug Lu

Qianmen Dajie

Zhushikou Dong Dajie

Huizhong

Tiantan Lu

wei
el

天坛

Temple of Heaven Park

Tiyuguan Lu

Tiantan Sportsmen's Inn

Longtan

Beijing

Park Hotel

facing today, while others retreat to a Taoist-inspired state of suspended animation, a long-sanctioned option in times of social instability. But it is clear that China's tentative opening to the West more than a decade ago has only accelerated the healthy quest for new values to replace those of a past now distorted beyond recognition, as China attempts to find a place for itself in the modern world.

Getting to Beijing

By Air

The number of direct flights to Beijing has increased dramatically in the past few years. A full list of airlines serving Beijing is given in Useful Addresses on page 191.

China's national airline, CAAC (the Civil Aviation Administration of China) has been decentralised. Air China now covers principal domestic routes and most international routes, while five regional airlines and CAAC cover remaining areas. Although part of an effort to improve airline service, standards have not improved radically and some confusion over ticketing and schedules has resulted.

Air China's main office is at 15 Xi Chang'an Jie (tel. 6017755), open 8 am–9 pm daily). Air China also has branches in the Beijing Hotel, the Lido Hotel and the Great Wall Sheraton. CITS and a few of the other agencies (see Useful Addresses page 191) will purchase airline tickets for you (for a small fee).

The most popular air route to Beijing from Hong Kong is on Dragonair. Flying time is just under three hours. Hong Kong Dragon Airlines Ltd (Dragonair)is located in Hong Kong at12 fl, Tower Six, China Hong Kong City, 33 Canton Road, Kowloon and in Beijing at L107, 1st fl, China World Trade Tower, 1 Jianguomenwai Dajie, Beijing 100004. When direct flights are full, there is an alternative route via Tianjin (on Air China) which adds one hour to the journey. Another possibility is to fly via Guangzhou (Canton) or Shanghai but obviously this takes longer.

Taxis are readily available at Beijing's Capital Airport and the fare to the city centre is around Rmb80–120. There is also an inexpensive bus available every half hour to Air China's main office in the centre of the city. The last bus from the airport leaves at 8 pm. A few hotels have an airport shuttle bus, and others will send a car if prearranged.

By Rail

Beijing can also be reached by train from Hong Kong, via Guangzhou. Through tickets may be booked in Hong Kong (around US$150 first-class), and the

journey takes 36 hours from Guangzhou. From Hong Kong to Guangzhou takes
around three hours. A first-, or 'soft', class sleeper on Chinese trains offers you
an old-fashioned, but comfortable, berth in a four-berth compartment, and
reasonable Chinese food in the restaurant car. If time is not a factor, this is an
interesting way to see China's richly varied countryside.

Once in Beijing, taxis are available at the railway station. The taxi stand is to
the right of the station exit.

Return rail tickets from Beijing cannot be bought outside China, but it is not
difficult to make the purchase in the capital. There is a special foreigners' ticket
office (tel. 5128931, hours 8 am–9 pm) at the rear of the main station central
hall, where the staff speak good English. Or, for a small additional fee, you may
ask a local travel agent, such as CITS, to buy it for you. Trains fill up fast, so
tickets should be booked several days in advance.

Foreigners are also permitted to travel to Beijing by train from Pyongyang,
from Ulan Bator on the trans-Mongolian railway, and from Moscow on the
trans-Siberian railway. But long-distance travel by road is not yet allowed for
foreigners in China.

Facts for the Traveller

Visas

Tourists travelling in a group enter China on a group visa—a single document
listing all members of the group. The visa is obtained by the tour operator on
behalf of his clients, and individual passports will not be stamped. Individual
visas can be obtained at Chinese embassies and consulates and perhaps certain
travel agencies in your respective countries; from the Chinese Ministry of
Foreign Affairs visa office in Hong Kong; or through several Hong Kong travel
agents including branches of CITS and CTS (see below). Just one passport
photograph and a completed application form are necessary. The visa gives you
automatic entry to the more than 500 open cities and areas in China.

Visa fees vary considerably depending on the source of the visa and on the
time taken to get it. In Hong Kong, for instance, you would pay around US$30
for a three-month visa granted within a few hours, while a standard one-month
tourist visa processed in three days will cost around US$20.

An application for a business visa should generally be accompanied by an
invitation from the appropriate host organization in China. In Hong Kong, all
that is needed is a letter from the applicant's company confirming that he wishes
to travel to China on business. Multiple re-entry visas are available for regular
business visitors.

Cursory Health Certificates must be filled in when crossing the border.
China's present policy does not require tourists or short-term residents to

provide proof of a negative AIDS test result. So far this has been limited to people staying in China for six months or longer. However, there has been some talk of making further restrictions. It would be wise to confirm their policy before arriving.

Customs

Visitors are required to fill out a customs declaration form, a duplicate of which must be kept and produced again when you leave. On this document you should list valuable personal possessions such as cameras, electrical appliances, watches and jewellery, as well as the total amount of foreign currency that you are taking into China. These listed items are not to be sold or given away while you are in China, and the customs officer may ask to see them when you leave. If you lose either the customs form or any of the items listed on it, you must report the loss to the Public Security Bureau. If you are unable to account for missing items you may be liable to a fine when you leave China.

Four bottles of alcohol, three cartons of cigarettes, unlimited film and unlimited medicines for personal use may be taken in. Firearms and dangerous drugs are strictly forbidden.

Antiques up to the value of Rmb10,000 may be taken out of China as long as each article bears a red wax seal which indicates that it may be exported. You are well advised to keep the relevant sales receipts for possible inspection at customs on departure.

Money

Chinese Currency

The Chinese currency is called 'Renminbi' (meaning 'people's currency') and this is abbreviated to Rmb. It is denominated in *yuan*, but referred to as *kuai* in everyday speech. The *yuan* is divided into ten *jiao* (colloquially called *mao*). Each *jiao* is in turn divided into 10 *fen*. There are large notes for 100, 50, 10, 5, 2, and 1 *yuan*, small notes for 5, 2 and 1 *jiao*, even smaller notes for 5, 2, and 1 *fen* and coins for 5, 2 and 1 *fen*.

Foreign Exchange Certificates

In exchange transactions,visitors are not given Rmb notes but Foreign Exchange Certificates (FEC or, in Chinese, *waihuijuan*). FECs were designed to be used by foreigners for payment in hotels, stores selling imported goods, and for taxis, airline tickets and international phone calls (foreign residents are issued with a 'yellow card' which permits them to use Rmb). FECs and Rmb (at heavy discount) can be reconverted (for which you will need to show exchange vouchers) when you leave China, but it is impossible to change them abroad.

Foreign Currency

There is no limit to the amount of foreign currency you can take into China. In the major cities, all freely negotiable currencies can be exchanged for FECs at branches of the Bank of China, in hotels and the large stores. If you need more cash during your stay, one way to get it is to have money wired in your name to the local main branch of the Bank of China. The remittance will arrive in four to six working days. A few credit card companies allow their card-holders to draw a cash advance of up to US$100 from the Bank of China. American Express card-holders may cash personal cheques for up to US$1,000 on payment of a charge. Otherwise, personal cheques, cashier's cheques and international money orders require 45 days' clearance.

Cheques and Credit Cards

All the major European, American and Japanese traveller's cheques are accepted. International credit cards may be used in a limited number of Friendship Stores, hotels and banks, and you should check with your credit card company or bank before you rely on this form of payment for your purchases.

Station to Station

ews was always passing, being digested and commented upon; and obviously it kept coming promptly and fresh from its source. This was specially true of the messengers who delivered "chits," the local name for our notes that replaced Western telephone calls. When foreigners were in close relation, such messengers might be on the road constantly. Each chit was entered into a chit-book (I have mine yet); and its receipt was attested, if the master was away from home, by a rubber stamp or else by the ordinary house seal pressed into it. The latter was esteemed more formal and therefore in better taste. If the message was received personally the master might scrawl his initials, foreign fashion, beside his own name. In this way we could nearly always tell quite accurately what had happened to every document.

When only a word of acknowledgement was needed, it was often added in this place. "Would you perhaps like to come picnicking on the lakes next Thursday evening?"—"With pleasure."—"Do you care to see the Devil Dancers tomorrow in the Lama Temple?"—Drop by my house first!"

These messengers came from other households; they were all known to each other; and they usually sat quietly in the kitchen, chatting and sipping tea while a return message was being devised within. Chits were often frisky; nearly everyone enjoyed the arrange-ment, not least the messenger himself. Sensing his role, he sat recounting the latest, or hearing our own news; and it never took long for anything of remark to spread over the town. A messenger with five notes to deliver knew by heart who had dined with whom the night before, how it had all gone, and so on, in the whole of his master's circle, by the time he returned home with his chit-book again. Further, since we were all said to have nicknames in these regions, the literal sentences must at times have been somewhat curious. One Westerner, who had a weakness for visiting hostesses just before meal hours, was known simply as the "Want-Food One." There were "Old Virgins" and Great or Small "Very-Verys" (older *or younger married women) in numbers.*

If that special rupture of the amenities commonly known as a "Peking quarrel" were bubbling, and they often did, the messenger's role would become more active. I do not know whether these altercations sprang from pride confronting pride, since on however small a scale each was sovereign in his own scrap of kingdom; or from exasperation when an adversary of one's own kind began to set bounds, to limit one's power. These were traits that life in courtyards engendered. Even the Chinese were aware of a common temptation to "bolt the door and set oneself up as Emperor."

Here I stumbled upon what must have been a wellspring of classical Chinese intrigue. Especially during love affairs, the messenger had a chance to make so much personal face, which he was not at all loath to seize, that drama sprang into being full-fledged. The household servants were informed: "As she wrote that chit, her amah *[maid] told me that she appeared to . . ." etc. This would be relayed within; and although I sternly discouraged such gossip, from time to time the situation would explode if my servants felt that I ought to know something of importance to myself (as they considered it), and therefore to all of us—before I penned my reply. After all they were my small army, and in the world ambush was inevitable. One must be prepared.*

Or perhaps some genial party was going forward, perhaps arrangements were being made in fine weather for an excursion to a distant temple; and the preparations—food, crockery, and transportation—were being divided. A message would come, and after domestic consultation I would select a sheet of paper. Finally I would put my envelope into the chit-book, adding on my line the words "Reply herewith." Meanwhile the messenger had kept his own liaison unbroken, sitting comfortably in the kitchen. The oral system worked quite as well, on his level, to keep him in touch with such affairs, as did for us our own writing. Connection was therefore double, and from the Chinese point of view now secure.

George N Kates, The Years that Were Fat
translated by William A Lyell

Tipping

Although China's tourism authorities have declared that tipping is forbidden, travellers may find that tour guides and taxi drivers, particularly those in major cities, are all too ready to accept tips.

Two-Tier Pricing

Unless you can read Chinese, you may not be aware that at many of the important tourist sights in Beijing, such as the Imperial Palace, Great Wall and Temple of Heaven, prices for locals and overseas tourists vary by as much as six to ten times. This is based on the principle that because the Chinese government subsidizes the leisure activities of the Chinese people, foreigners should subsidize the Chinese government—and this is becoming increasingly questionable— they should pay comparably more when they are travelling in China.

Many Chinese are surprised to learn that no such system operates in the West. But what is wrong with this basically racist system is that anyone who the ticket seller thinks is Chinese—and that could include Koreans, Taiwanese, Hong Kong people, as well as Overseas Chinese from Switzerland—can buy a cheap ticket. This privilege also extends to anyone who speaks Chinese with reasonable fluency. As the generally laid back ticket sellers rarely look at the person buying the tickets through the tiny (for sanitary reasons) ticket window, anyone who asks for a ticket in Mandarin Chinese is likely to be sold one at the local price.

Local Time

The whole of China operates within one time zone. Beijing time is eight hours ahead of GMT and 13 hours ahead of EST. It also adopts summer time, when clocks are moved forward by one hour. Summer time begins on the first Sunday of April and ends on the first Sunday in September.

Packing Checklist

The electricity supply is 220 volts and the sockets are mostly two-pin. Take a selection of adaptors for your electrical appliances but you may not be able to use them at all outside of the larger cities. Many brands of toiletries, taken for granted in the West, are not widely available in China, so plan to be self-sufficient in such necessities as toothpaste, shaving cream, razor blades, shampoo, sanitary towels and tampons. It is also wise to bring along sufficient supplies of any prescription medicines you are taking, and an extra pair of prescription glasses, if only to save time and trouble, if you lose or break them.

Communications

Telecommunications

Beijing's local telephone system has too few lines so making a local call can be time-consuming and frustrating. An additional complication has resulted from the current telecommunication expansion programme which has involved changing many of Beijing's telephone numbers.

Local phone calls can be so distorted by static they sound like a jammed radio broadcast, while international calls are usually as clear as crystal. No secret message here, simply a question of rusty old wires versus shiny new satellites.

Your hotel may be able to help you find up-to-date numbers. Or you could try dialling information on 114 (local calls), or 116 (long-distance). *The China Phone Book,* published in Hong Kong, and available in some hotels in China, is the best source for business telephone numbers.

Most major hotels now offer International Direct Dialling (IDD) to dozens of countries, and domestic long-distance calls have become much easier through a direct dialling service established at the end of 1987. To place a call, you either fill out a form which you then give to the floor staff or simply dial the hotel operator and provide the phone number and place which you want to call.

There is a 24-hour telecommunication office at Xidan, for telephone calls, cables and telexes. Other Post and Telecommunications offices are given in Useful Addresses on page 191.

Vital Telephone Numbers

China international dialling code	86
Beijing international dialling code	861
Beijing Emergency Centre	120
Beijing directory inquiries	114
International operator	115
Domestic long-distance operator	113
Domestic long-distance inquiry	116
Time (in Chinese)	117
Weather (in Chinese)	121
Beijing suburban operator	118
Tourist Hotline	5130828

Hutongs

Beijing's *hutongs*—backalleys—are where Chinese life can be seen at its most typical and traditional.

Mostly doomed to be torn down and redeveloped for modern housing blocks, these fascinating little streets form a miniature grid of walled courtyards and passage ways, in between the sweeping boulevards which are the main traffic arteries.

Often blessed with picturesque names—Knitting Yarn Hutong, Sea Transport Granary Hutong, Performing Music Hutong, Little Trumpet Hutong and Big Trumpet Hutong–the *hutongs* are essentially residential areas where the informality of ordinary life can be witnessed. Pot plants nod at the visitor passing by, and a canary in a cage mocks the rare cat which slinks over an old, grey-plastered wall. Old men dawdle with their long-stemmed pipes, and grandma takes the well-padded baby out for a stroll.

There is much debate about the origin of the word *hutong*. The most convincing argument is that *hutong* derives from a Mongol word, 'hotlog', that means 'water well' and suggests a small geographical area of the city that may have been served by

a single well. It is likely that during the Yuan dynasty, when the Mongols established their capital Dadu in an area that generally coincides with the limits of the later Ming and Qing capitals, they dug many wells. However as most of the well water was brackish, and eventually proved insufficient for the growing city's needs, canals were dug to supply the city with water from several sources in the western suburbs and link up the Grand Canal to the urban waterway system. In this way the imperial granaries could be filled directly from the barges that transported tribute rice from southern China, whereas transhipment had previously been necessary.

The names of some Beijing *hutongs* have changed several times, including a major anti-feudal whitewashing during the Cultural Revolution. One choice example from that period can be rendered in English as 'Red-to-the-end-of-the *Hutong.*'

Sometimes a commune donkey-car loaded with vegetables seeks passage along the narrow lanes, and teenagers loaf around joking. The walls are daubed with slogans such as 'Observe Hygiene' and 'Look After Soldiers' Families Well' but the air of perpetual afternoon overpowers propaganda.

Nearly every hotel in Beijing has a fax machine and offers the service for a three-minute minimum charge. After adding the service charge, which can range from 10 to as much as 30 percent, the minimum cost for sending a fax to Hong Kong is around Y40 and overseas around Y60. Most hotels also charge a small fee for receiving faxes.

Many hotels have telex machines, but not necessarily operators to assist you in punching the tape.

Several international courier services now operate out of Beijing and the other major Chinese cities. Their addresses and those of other Post and Telecommunications offices are given in Useful Addresses on page 191.

English-language Media

The English-language Chinese newspaper, *China Daily*, began publication in mid-1981 and is available at all hotel magazine kiosks. *Newsweek, Time* and a number of international magazines, newspapers and paperback novels are also on sale at hotels or at the Foreign Languages Bookstore in Wangfujing. The Chinese themselves publish magazines about China in English as well as books on a wide variety of subjects, some political, some not. Hong Kong publications such as *The South China Morning Post, The Asian Wall Street Journal* and the *Far Eastern Economic Review* are usually available in many of the hotels, often late in the afternoon of the date of publication.

Travel Agencies

Travellers to China will almost certainly come across the State-owned China International Travel Service (CITS) or China Travel Service (CTS), which at one time had the monopoly of handling arrangements for all visitors, with CITS being responsible for foreigners, and CTS taking care of overseas Chinese. Although there are now 18 approved travel agencies that may issue visas and deal directly with foreign tour operators, CITS/CTS remain the largest travel organizations in the country. CITS/CTS services cover accommodation, transport, food, sightseeing, interpreters and special tours, as well as ticket sales for individual walk-in customers.

The Beijing Tourist Bureau has set up a **tourist hotline**, with operators who speak English, Japanese and Chinese. The number is 5130828.

Climate and Clothing

Beijing has four clearly defined seasons. From November to March, winter is usually dry and clear but winds from the northwest can bring temperatures down to -15.5°C (-4°F). In November and the first half of December, the weather is crisp and cool and the cerulean blue of the sky intensifies to the point where it appears like a vast turquoise lens. Locals describe the early winter sky as 'tall' or 'high' or 'deep'. The best winter clothing is layers of warm garments including thermal underwear, sweaters and coats, in addition to warm boots and fur hats with earflaps. Heating in the hotels can be very fierce, while heating in some public buildings can be inadequate or nonexistent. China follows a system of 'command heating'. North of the Yangtze, the heat in many public buildings and residences is turned on 15 November and turned off 15 March, regardless of the temperature. And in many local apartment buildings, the heat goes on for a few hours in the morning and is turned off during the day to conserve fuel. The Chinese produce good winter clothing such as thick cotton underwear, padded jackets and furs, all at reasonable prices.

Spring usually lasts from mid March to mid May and is a good time for a visit, with trees and flowers coming into bloom and the occasional shower to wash the city. Clothing should include a warm coat and sweaters as well as some light-weight clothes, and possibly a raincoat.

Late spring, from mid-March to early May is the season for Beijing's notorious dust storms which have a history of several hundred years. They don't blow in every year, but when they do you know it. The atmosphere is filled with a near-pudding of yellow to orange dust from the Gobi Desert to the west that finds its way into everything from sealed closets to your closed mouth. No amount of tree planting seems to be able to reduce the amount or density of the dust. It is generally dusty in Beijing whenever it is dry.

Beijing summers are very hot and humid. Temperatures reach 40°C (104°F) and rainfall is light. Light, cotton clothing is recommended. Visitors will often be in places without air-conditioning.

Autumn is the best season in the capital. From September to mid October it is warm, sunny and dry. There is a wealth of colour in the parks, and fruit and flowers in the markets. Dress as you would for autumn in southern Europe or northern California.

Beijing has a large diplomatic community of approximately 20,000, including dependents, and about the same number of resident business people, so to that extent it is more formal than other Chinese cities. The Chinese do not mind whether visitors dress formally or informally, as long as they are neat and do not show too much flesh. Beijing youth are now carrying out some bold experiments in fashion and hair design, as Chinese society gradually opens up to the outside world.

Average Temperatures in Beijing

		C°	F°		C°	F°		C°	F°
Average		-4.4	24.1		18.9	66.0		19.1	66.4
High	JAN	1.7	35.1	MAY	25.3	77.5	SEP	25.5	77.9
Low		-9.7	14.5		11.9	53.4		12.2	53.8
Average		-2.1	28.2		23.9	74.5		12.2	53.9
High	FEB	3.8	38.8	JUN	29.6	85.3	OCT	18.7	65.7
Low		-7.2	19.0		17.7	63.9		6.8	44.2
Average		4.7	40.5		52.6	78.1		4.3	39.7
High	MAR	11.0	51.8	JUL	30.3	86.5	NOV	10.0	50.0
Low		-0.9	30.4		21.5	70.7		-0.2	31.6
Average		13.0	55.4		24.0	75.2		-2.5	27.5
High	APR	19.4	66.9	AUG	28.9	84.0	DEC	3.0	37.4
Low		6.5	43.7		19.9	67.8		-7.0	19.4

Health

China has no specific requirements regarding vaccinations for visitors, however since 1990 any foreign citizen planning to live in China for a period of six months or more was requested to present the result of an AIDS test. Similarly Chinese citizens who have lived abroad for more than six months were given a compulsory AIDS test (and charged about US$50 for it) before being admitted to the country.

Consult a physician or a government health authority (in the USA, the US State Department) for their recommendations on vaccinations for China. In recent years, the US Consulate in Hong Kong has suggested hepatitis B, gama globulin (for hepatitis A), Japanese B encephalitis (not available in the USA), tetanus, polio, cholera and malaria. However this terrifying list should be considered alongside the specifics of your itinerary. For a fall trip to Beijing, Xi'an, Shanghai, Suzhou and Guilin, the possibility of contracting any of these diseases is minuscule. It is only when travelling to southwest China in the summer or to very out of the way areas that a regimen should be considered. Long term residents in Beijing often take the series of innoculations against encephalitis, a mosquito-borne disease.

Peking Versus Beijing: What's in a Name?

First, let's learn to pronounce the name of the city. *Bei* sounds like 'bay' with the B pronounced softer than an English B, but harder than a P; and *jing* sounds like the second syllable of 'paging' or 'staging'—there is a bit of friction in the initial consonant. The j in Beijing is *not* the equivalent of a French soft g, as in *gardin* or *leger*.

'Peking' is the English version of the earlier French Pekin (also a city in Ohio).

Until the 1970s, nearly all English publications used the 19th-century Wade Giles romanization system to render Chinese names in English, except in the case of certain place names which used the French-influenced postal spellings, such as Amoy (for Hsia-men or Xiamen), Chekiang (for Che-chiang or Zhejiang), Chungking (for Ch'ung-ch'ing or Chongqing), and Tientsin (for T'ian-chin or Tianjin).

In the early 1970s, when China began to dance its first tentative tango with the outside world, and the names of Chinese people and places began to appear in foreign newspapers, China adopted its own *pinyin* romanization system and pronounced it official. *Pinyin* literally 'spell the sounds', had been developed in China based on the Russian cyrillic alphabet, hence its eye-crossing x's, zh's and q's not followed by u's. *Pinyin* is less unwieldy than Wade Giles, but like any romanization system, depends more on the inner ear than the eye. Most of the world adopted the *pinyin* spellings for Chinese place names, but some newspapers and publishers braved the pedantic push from Beijing to promote the *pinyin* spelling of a city that to anglophones has been Peking for about 300 years. What would happen if the Italians asked us to write Roma, and the Spaniards Espana? Some orthodox Chinese pedants went so far as to suggest changing China to *Zhongguo*, as the name of that great country is written in *pinyin*. '*China* isn't a Chinese word' they say, 'it was forced down our throats by foreigners.' Shall we then have a Zhongguoish meal at a Zhongguoish restaurant where the waiters only speak Zhongguonese?

Asian libraries throughout the world were also thrown into a quandary about how to catalogue their Chinese books, and some of the great Chinese libraries in the west have two separate card systems, one for *pinyin* and one for Wade Giles. As card catalogues are computerized, the difficulties will lessen.

The most common ailments contracted by tourists in China are upper respiratory infections, in other words, chest colds. Some physicians prescribe a quarter-dose of an antibiotic like tetracycline as a mild preventative. Beijing is extremely dry and cold in the winter, and it is necessary to dress well and drink lots of fluids all the time. Beijing residents tend to dress much more warmly than seems necessary during the transitional seasons of fall and spring, and are often amazed to see foreigners wearing short sleeves and short pants when they are still wearing long underwear. Chinese people seem to believe that overdressing is the key to staying healthy during these seasons.

Never drink unboiled water in Beijing, and if you are a purist, try to avoid rinsing your mouth with tap water, using instead the water in the thermos in your hotel room. Because Chinese standards of sanitation lag behind those of the West—for instance, China's national sport, spitting, and the habit of children urinating and defecating in the streets—it makes good sense to wash your hands carefully before eating anything. Peel all fruit and avoid raw leafy vegetables unless you are in an upmarket restaurant.

Beijing has a number of hospitals for foreigners, emergency clinics, and international medical evacuation offices. (See the listings in Useful Addresses, page 191.) The medical emergency telephone number is 120. If you are in a hotel, tell the front desk that you need an ambulance. Several hospitals have emergency services for foreigners.

> Peking Union Medical College Hospital (PUMC) *Xie he yi yuan*
> (comprehensive hospital with a large clinic for foreigners)
> Dongdan Beidajie
> Tel. 5127733
>
> Sino-Japanese Friendship Hospital *Zhong Ri you hao yi yuan*
> Hepingli Beijie
> Tel. 4221122
>
> Sino-German Policlinic *Zhong De zhen suo* (privately run 24-hour
> ambulance service; performs minor surgery)
> Basement, Landmark Tower, 8 Dong Sanhuanlu
> Tel. 5011983, 5016688 extn. 20903
>
> Beijing Friendship Hospital
> Yong'an Lu, Tianqiao
> Tel. 3014411

It is impossible to generalize about the quality of Chinese medical services, but in Beijing doctors tend to be thorough and reliable, particularly in geriatric medicine; just think of all the octegenarians thay have to keep on their feet! Most long-term foreign residents, however, prefer to travel abroad for major medical and dental treatment.

A handful of foreign embassies provide limited medical service for their own nationals, but as a rule embassy medical staff are not permitted to practice in Chinese hospitals, and thus they should be brought into emergencies on a consulting basis only.

Getting Around

Most visitors use taxis to get around Beijing. Other forms of transport can turn out to be more of an adventure than a rapid means of getting to a particular destination on time.

According to municipal statistics, there are over 200 taxi companies in operation with as many as 9,000 cars. Taxis range from Chinese-style curtained limousines to racy Peugeots, Toyotas or Mercedes. During the day there are usually plenty of taxis at the places frequented by foreigners—outside major hotels, sights, office buildings, restaurants. But if you stray off the normal tourist track, it is safer to ask the taxi to wait. The charge involved is small, but during the busy tourist season, the driver may refuse to do so. In this case, you could call the English-speaking central office of the Capital (Shoudu) Car Company— tel. 5321044—and they should send a taxi for you. Some taxis respond to being hailed in the street, while others do not.

In 1991, taxi rates were Rmb1.20–2.00 a kilometre (0.6 mile) for better cars. Taxis may also be hired for a day, or half day. Your hotel should be able to arrange this. The cost was Rmb250 a day in 1991.

Nearly all taxis have working metres, with different settings on them for day, night and out of town trips. A 50 percent premium is added to the tab—and appears on the metre—if your ride exceeds 15 kilometres (10 miles).

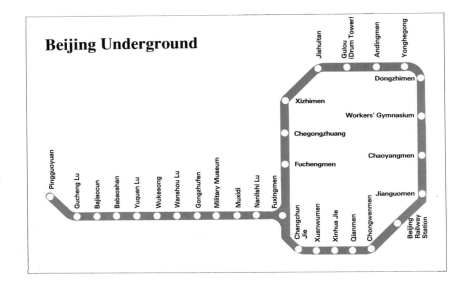

Beijing Underground

Stations shown: Pingguoyuan, Gucheng Lu, Bajiaocun, Babaoshan, Yuquan Lu, Wukesong, Wanshou Lu, Gongzhufen, Military Museum, Muxidi, Nanlishi Lu, Fuxingmen, Changchun Jie, Xuanwumen, Xinhua Jie, Qianmen, Chongwenmen, Beijing Railway Station, Jianguomen, Chaoyangmen, Workers' Gymnasium, Dongzhimen, Yonghegong, Andingmen, Gulou (Drum Tower), Jishuitan, Xizhimen, Chegongzhuang, Fuchengmen

Following a few years when the newspapers and taxi companies received a spate of complaints from both foreigners and locals about how taxi drivers were overcharging, the taxi industry seems to have cleaned up its act. This improvement in service came in the wake of several murders of taxi drivers, although the motive of these killings is not clear.

You will be offered a hand written receipt after every ride. However, if you are willing to forego the receipt, it is possible to strike a deal with the driver (mutual benefit and all that) and pay less than the metre rate—under the critical condition that the driver does not turn on the metre. It is probably best to ask for the receipt up front if you are given the choice until you know the territory.

The Beijing underground subway system has connected what were formerly two lines. One must purchase a 50 *fen* ticket for any destination. The only transfer station is at Fuxingmen. Stations are named in *pinyin*, so are recognizable even if you do not read Chinese characters.

Buses and trolleybuses are more difficult to handle for newcomers to the city, partly because of the dense, pushing, crowds that use them at most times of day and night, but also because fares are based on the distance you intend to travel. If you cannot speak Chinese, get someone to write down your destination to show the ticket collector. The collector might also help you get off at the right spot. A map showing the capital's complex bus and trolleybus system is usually available in hotel bookstores. Buses in the city costs 10 *fen* for 1–6 stops and 20 *fen* for 7–12 stops.

When riding buses in Beijing, make sure you have small change in renminbi notes or coins. Busfares range from 10 to 30 *fen*. If you hand the ticketseller an FEC10 note, you are bound to get a fistful of small Rmb notes in change. It is also wise to watch your pockets and pocketbooks on public transport and in crowded places. Thieves sometimes cut open tourists' bags with a sharp blade and extract the contents. Independent tourists should keep their cash, tickets and passport in a money belt or a hanging pouch worn around the neck and under the clothing.

From 8 am–5 pm there are 'mini-buses' available which cover long distances in the city at minimal expense. There are four routes covering different sections of Beijing (passengers can disembark at any point): 1. Train station to Beihai Park via Wangfujing and the Forbidden City. 2. Train Station to Beijing Zoo. 3. Beijing Zoo to the Summer Palace. 4. Train Station to Yongdingmen station in the south of Beijing.

The buses run every 15–30 minutes along these routes; they can be hailed on the streets but the easiest place to find them is at Qianmen Gate. The fare is Rmb1–5 depending on the distance one travels.

A more adventurous way for energetic tourists to see the city is by bicycle. There are a number of bicycle hire shops used to catering to foreigners. One which is conveniently located is the Jianguomenwai Bicycle Repair Shop, just across the street from the Friendship Store. It is open 7.30 am–6 pm and a bicycle costs Rmb5 a day. Another is Limin, at 2 Chongwenmenwai Dajie, not far from the Xinqiao Hotel.

Entertainment

Few aspects of Beijing life have changed so dramatically in recent years as the sudden mushrooming of amenities for foreigners. Of course, the city's offerings are still meagre compared with most Asian capitals, but there are more diversions for foreign visitors than five years back when the only evening possibilities were cultural shows, or banquets which tended to wind up before 8 pm. Now Beijing offers comfortable bars, pleasant restaurants where you can enjoy a leisurely meal, health centres, swimming pools, 24-hour coffee shops, discos, and bowling alleys.

It is Beijing's new foreign-managed hotels that have been largely responsible for spicing up the capital's leisure time, and this is where the best facilities are to be found.

Nightlife

In order to keep up with the Jones and the Zhangs, every new joint venture hotel in Beijing has its own bar, disco and often karaoke set up. The only problem with bar-hopping in Beijing is that some of the distances between bars are vast.

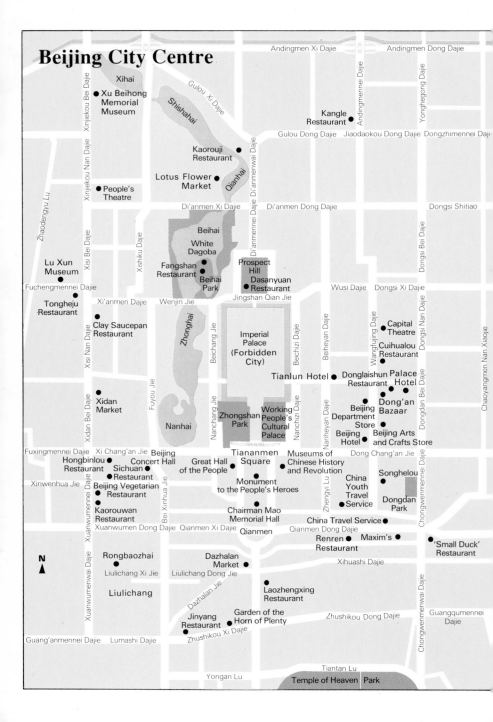

Beijing City Centre

Andingmen Xi Dajie   Andingmen Dong Dajie

Xihai

Xu Beihong Memorial Museum

Gulou Xi Dajie

Shishahai

Xinjiekou Bei Dajie

Andingmennei Dajie

Yonghegong Dajie

Kangle Restaurant

Gulou Dong Dajie   Jiaodaokou Dong Dajie   Dongzhimennei Daji

Kaorouji Restaurant

Lotus Flower Market

Qianhai

Di'anmennei Dajie

Di'anmenwai Dajie

Xinjiekou Nan Dajie

People's Theatre

Di'anmen Xi Dajie   Di'anmen Dong Dajie

Dongsi Shitiao

Zhaodengyu Lu

Beihai

White Dagoba

Xishiku Dajie

Xisi Bei Dajie

Dongsi Bei Dajie

Lu Xun Museum

Fangshan Restaurant

Beihai Park

Prospect Hill

Dasanyuan Restaurant

Fuchengmennei Dajie

Jingshan Qian Jie

Wusi Dajie   Dongsi Xi Dajie

Tongheju Restaurant

Xi'anmen Dajie   Wenjin Jie

Zhonghai

Behai Dajie

Beichang Jie

Beichizi Dajie

Behai Dajie

Behan Dajie

Dongsi Nan Dajie

Clay Saucepan Restaurant

Xisi Nan Dajie

Imperial Palace (Forbidden City)

Wangfujing Dajie

Capital Theatre

Cuihualou Restaurant

Chaoyangmen Nan Xiaojie

Xidan Bei Dajie

Xidan Market

Fuyou Jie

Tianlun Hotel

Donglaishun Restaurant

Palace Hotel

Dong'an Bazaar

Dongdan Bei Dajie

Nanhai

Zhongshan Park

Working People's Cultural Palace

Nanchang Jie

Nanchizi Dajie

Nanheyan Dajie

Beijing Department Store

Beijing Hotel

Dong'an Bazaar

Beijing Arts and Crafts Store

Fuxingmennei Dajie   Xi Chang'an Jie

Beijing Concert Hall

Tiananmen Square

Dong Chang'an Jie

Hongbinlou Restaurant

Sichuan Restaurant

Great Hall of the People

Museums of Chinese History and Revolution

Songhelou

Dongwenmennei Dajie

Xinwenhua Jie

Beijing Vegetarian Restaurant

Bei Xinhua Jie

Monument to the People's Heroes

China Youth Travel Service

Dongdan Park

Kaorouwan Restaurant

Xuanwumennei Dajie

Xuanwumen Dong Dajie   Qianmen Xi Dajie

Chairman Mao Memorial Hall

Qianmen

Zhengyi Lu

China Travel Service

Qianmen Dong Dajie

Renren Restaurant

Maxim's

'Small Duck' Restaurant

Rongbaozhai

Dazhalan Market

Xihuashi Dajie

Liulichang Xi Jie   Liulichang Dong Jie

Chongwenmenwai Dajie

Liulichang

Dazhalan Jie

Laozhengxing Restaurant

Jinyang Restaurant

Garden of the Horn of Plenty

Zhushikou Dong Dajie

Guangqumennei Dajie

Guang'anmennei Dajie   Lumashi Dajie

Zhushikou Xi Dajie

Yongan Lu

Tiantan Lu

Temple of Heaven Park

N

Sadly, the ground floor lounge in the East Wing of the **Beijing Hotel**, has been converted to a shopping area, and so the famous people watching (medical students from Upper Volta flirting in Chinese with French backpackers as Hungarian plumbing equipment dealers and Japanese traders looked on) that used to take place here has moved several hundred metres down the hollow corridor to the rather confined and confining bar—it is literally behind a railing—in the West Wing of the hotel. This is a centralized place to meet in totally unpretentious surroundings where the nostalgia is thick. The service here has that ineffable patina of laid back insouciance that adheres to the modern Beijing waiter like the mossy green of an ancient bronze vessel.

The British-style **Red Lion** pub sits atop the **China World Tower,** and on the ground floor of the west wing office building there is a German-style **Brauhaus.** For the adventurous, the **Mediterranean Island** bar on an island in Qianhai Lake, north of Beihai Park is a laid back place in a splendid setting.

In the evening, a favourite place to go for a cocktail is **Charlie's Bar** in the Jianguo Hotel. An established feature of this bar are the nightly specials offering pizza, tacos and curries on various nights of the week. Frequented by Beijing's foreign correspondents and resident business community, this friendly bar is usually quite active. To a lesser extent the same is true of the **Jinglun's bar** next door.

At **Maxim's** lavishly ornate bar (2 Qianmen Xi Lu), which serves drinks to non-diners after 9 pm, the atmosphere is more intimate and reserved. Here one finds a taste of *la belle epoque* within China. Occasionally, Maxim's sponsors Saturday night dances where perfume, pearls and silk are suddenly *de rigueur* rather than conspicuously out of place.

For nightly dancing, there are several discos which stay open as late as 2 am. **Juliana's** at the **Holiday Inn Lido** is a popular place to dance for Beijing's diplomatic and expatriate community, particularly younger people. Other popular discos are **Rumours** at the **Palace Hotel**, **Talk of the Town** at the **China World Hotel,** and the hi-tech **Faces** in the **Jing Ghuang New World Hotel**. The Yanshan Hotel (in the Haidian district) disco is popular with foreign students and often presents local bands. Admission charge at these places averages FEC30.

Shangri-La's Xanadu disco tends to attract an older, quieter clientele to its richly furnished disco. The music is softer and its lighting more monochromatic. Most guests are likely to be on short-term business trips. A dress code does not allow blue jeans or sneakers inside (entry Rmb25).

For karaoke fans, the karaoke lounge in the **Jing Guang New World Hotel** features a huge video screen. Two other karaoke venues are **The Point After** at the **Palace Hotel** and the karaoke lounge in the **Kunlun Hotel**. Numerous karaoke bars patronized by the locals are spread throughout the city, many of them featuring Chinese revolutionary songs.

An upmarket place featuring live music is the **Cosmos Club** at the **Great Wall Sheraton**. Five days a week many people from Beijing's resident business community dance to the music of an imported Filipino band. One Saturday each month, the Cosmos Club offers a dinner dance which includes a cocktail, dinner and dancing.

If you are interested in a place where you can comfortably pass the evening in conversation or private contemplation either the lobby lounge at the Shangri-la or the atrium lobby at the Great Wall Sheraton offer elegant settings, attentive service and musical accompaniment. There are also several places with panoramic views of the city. The newly opened revolving French restaurant on the top floor of the Kunlun Hotel offers bar service in the evening. Across the street, the Great Wall Sheraton also features a first floor lounge, but the local favourite is the **Sky Lounge** at the Windows-on the-World in the Citic building. The rooftop café at the Beijing Hotel attracts lively crowds in the summer.

The venerable Beijing institution of the teahouse has been revived on the third floor of a commercial building in the Qianmen area, two doors to the west of Kentucky Fried Chicken. This is the **Lao She Teahouse**, named after the famous Beijing author of *Rickshaw Boy*, who was murdered or committed suicide in Beijing during the Cultural Revolution. Here from 3.30 to 5 pm and 7.30 to 9 pm every night, there are performances by traditional Beijing ballad singers, story tellers, conjurors and masters of cross-talk, a two-person comedy routine. Snacks and tea are served. Booking is advisable for the evening (tel. 546324) although the teahouse is open from 9 am to 9pm. Address: Building 3, Qianmenxi Dajie.

Sports

The largest, most pleasant, outdoor pool open to foreigners is at the **Friendship Hotel**. This is open June–September. **Great Wall Sheraton** has a small leisure pool (indoor/outdoor) and a health club, open 7 am–10 pm, complete with gym, sauna, whirlpool and steam-baths, as well as aerobics sessions. (For non-residents an all-inclusive entry fee is Rmb36, or less if you select one or two facilities.) Swimming and gym wear may be hired. There are also tennis courts here, as well as massage and acupuncture. (Annual membership is US$400, which gives unlimited use of all sports facilities.) The **Shangri-La** was fully opened in 1987, offering another top-quality pool and health club in the city.

Chinese massage and acupuncture are, of course, much more widely offered than western-style health facilities in Beijing's hotels, and the charges are more reasonable.

The **Holiday Inn Lido**'s sports complex (which includes indoor/outdoor tennis courts, jacuzzi, pool, gym squash, bowling) is the largest in Beijing. This is for members only (tel. 5006688 ext. 2882), but non-residents may use the heated swimming pool, sauna and health club. The **Fragrant Hills Hotel** also has a good health centre, but it is long way to travel if you are staying in the city centre.

Bowling alleys can be found at the **Holiday Inn Lido, Beijing International Hotel, Xin Da Du Hotel**, and **Tianlun Dynasty Hotel**.

The **International Club**, in Jianguomen, had its heyday when it was one of the few places foreign residents could go. Although clientele has fallen off, the club still has activities for foreign visitors. Its two tennis courts are much in demand, so reserve ahead if you go (tel. 5322046). Costs are Rmb40 an hour daytime, Rmb65 an hour at night. There are expensive Chinese and western restaurants at the club, which anyone may use.

For golfers, there is the impressive **Beijing International Golf Club**, dramatically set in the Ming Tombs area. The course was designed by Japan Golf Promotions as part of a Sino-Japanese joint venture. Visitor fees are Rmb450 weekdays, and Rmb600 at weekends and national holidays. The luxurious complex includes a clubhouse, reception hall and guesthouse. Contact the club at Qianmen Hotel (tel. 3016688 ext. 4021 or 3013434).

The **Beijing Recreation Centre** is an entire sports complex, with bowling, squash, tennis, roller skating, disco, billiards, and a sauna. It is located at Beisihuanzhong Lu, Andingmenwai, near the east gate of the Asian Games Village. Tel. 4993434–6.

The **North China International Shooting Academy** offers riflemen the ultimate in shooting satisfaction. China's Ministry of Defence set up this shooting range in 1987 near Badaling to help finance the military. Visitors can pay to shoot anything from handguns and machine guns (Rmb5 per shot) to such heavy-weight weapons as anti-aircraft guns and even rocket-propelled grenade launchers (Rmb560 per shot). The shooting range is open daily from 8 am–5 pm (tel. 301357).

Major spectator sports events are usually held at the **Workers' Stadium** (Gongren Tiyuchang) in the northeast of the city. CITS should be able to tell you what is on, and get tickets. Soccer, table-tennis, basketball, volleyball and gymnastic events, are very popular.

Beijing now has two amusement parks. **Nine Dragon Amusement Park** is located on the shores of the Ming Tombs Reservoir in Miyun County, approximately 75 kilometres (47 miles) from Beijing. The park has the makings of a Chinese Disneyland, and some of the hardware used in the Underwater Dragon Palace, with nine scenes reproducing key figures from Chinese mythology, are imported from the USA. There are numerous restaurants, a swimming pool, and boating facilities on the reservoir. The park is a Chinese-Japanese joint venture built at a cost of US$35 million. For information on opening hours, tel. 3014926.

Another amusement park based on a dragon theme is **Longtanhu (Dragon Lake) Park** south of Longtan Lu directly east of the Temple of Heaven. A number of the imported rides will be familiar to amusement park goers.

There is a small children's amusement park on the eastern shore of Beihai lake in Beihai Park.

Noble House

P ao's home and mine were in the same street in Peking, a half-street that ambled leisurely along the bank of a canal in the Forbidden City: on the one side blank, secret walls and roofed gatewaays flanked by curled and grinning carved stone lions; on the other side the willows and the water. Pao's house was very important, much the richest and most noble in our street. Great gates opened upon a vista through courtyard after courtyard, spacious, imposing. Pillared pavilions supported wide roofs that swept in stately curves against the sky. Gold leaf and lacquer and deep-cut carving made splendid the doors and pillars. My home at the far end of the short street was quite modest by comparison—a single courtyard surrounded by small, unpretentious rooms.

This great house of Pao's family was in a continual stir of magnificent activity, fascinating to all the children in our street. We would gather about the gateway, watching, listening. It was a pageant for our benefit and we missed none of it. In the morning we came running to see the departure of Pao's father for the yamen, where the government offices were. The mounted body-guard would be drawn up at the gates, waiting. The lord of the house would issue forth, take his place in his carriage, and drive away, with the solemn clatter of many hoofs accompanying him.

Later in the forenoon came merchants. It might be a slender, smart young clerk, carrying some small and valuable parcel. It might be the proprietor of a shop himself, plump and prosperous, idly wafting his fan, followed by apprentices loaded with bundles and boxes. For the women of this household preferred not to soil their satin shoes, running about the streets. They lived for the most part secluded within their own inner courtyards, and when they wished to purchase anything—whether silks, or thin porcelain bowls and cups, or ear-rings of silver-gilt set with jade or coral—a selection was brought for their choice.

At noon in the winter we watched the "doing of good works". Files of the poor and beggars would come on the hour as though summoned. *They would stand at the gates with their cracked bowls and pots, waiting for the gift of food each day distributed. The stewards of the household then came out, carrying huge crocks of jow, the soft-cooked rice, steaming in the frosty air. They would ladle out the jow into the bowls held out to them by gaunt and dirty hands, and the beggars would warm their hands on the bowls as they sucked up the scalding hot rice.*

Most dazzling of all the glories of Pao's house, to the watching children, were feast nights, when guests came riding to the gates in rickshaws and four-wheeled open carriages, all tinkling with bells on the harness, with footmen attending before and behind. We edged into the outer courtyards, as close as we might come to the centre of festivity in the high court beyond. Here we could see and hear and even smell of things sumptuous, as gorgeously robed ladies passed us almost close enough to touch, smelling of flowers and sandalwood and musk; and hurrying servants crossed and recrossed the courtyard bearing great bowls and platters that left on the air a trail of exquisite savour to make the mouth water.

Creeping still closer we would watch, enchanted, the actors brought to entertain the company, the best in Peking (and that meant the best in China!). Emperors and heros of long-ago dynasties came to life in their song and pantomine, to the brazen music of gongs and cymbals, the intricate beat of drums, the shrill quaver of stringed instruments. We knew by heart each play and legend; we hailed by name the characters as they appeared, recognizing Tsao-Tsao by his treacherous, skull-white face and loyal Kung by his green robe and scarlet complexion, and the clowns with a tiny white patch over the bridge of the nose. Before a word was spoken we knew what scene was to be played. We were endlessly fascinated by the gold-encrusted robes, the helmets plumbed with yard-long pheasant feathers. And even to us, children though we were, there was significance and beauty in the stylized acting. There was excitement and meaning in the dance combat with spears and swords whirling, gowns and pheasant feathers whirling, drums and cymbals clashing, lights glancing gold and violet and crimson over the rich embroidered robes. . . .

Han Suyin, Destination Chungking

Performing Arts

Although there is a wide variety of cultural performances in Beijing it is sometimes difficult to find out what is on. There is not always a discernible regularity
in performances, nor is there a special 'What's On' publication in English. The
visitor simply has to ask around on arrival in the city.

As well as the traditional Chinese arts of opera, music and acrobatics, there
is a broadening range of performances of western music, theatre and ballet,
along with occasional visits from major foreign performers. Some CITS and
CTS staff may tell you which shows are on, and purchase the ticket for you,
but others may prove less helpful. There is a comprehensive listing of cultural
events in the *China Daily* but it is essential to phone the venue and find out if
tickets are available.

In the case of well known international performers, nearly all the tickets are
distributed to key work units, such as the military and the police—who attend in

uniform, of course—and other higher ups, as well as to the embassy of the country of the performer's origin, the music school (if it is a musician), etc. . . . You didn't come all the way to China to hear Pavaroti did you?

Thus buying tickets can be a trying business in Beijing. Tickets for just about everything sell out fast, and some box offices are not keen to sell tickets to foreigners. It is best to try and get someone else to do the queuing for you.

Acrobatics

Acrobatic troupes, whose amazing skills derive from a long tradition of street theatre, stage highly sophisticated performances. Many of their best-known acts have a timeless appeal—the 'Pagoda of Bowls', 'Plate Spinning' and 'Handstand upon a Pyramid of Chairs' amongst them. Acrobatics shows may be performed at the **Capital Gymnasium** (Shoudu Tiyuguan), the **Workers' Gymnasium** (Gongren Tiyuchang), and **Beijing Gymnasium** (Beijing Tiyuguan). The city's best-known acrobatics troupes are the China Acrobatics Troupe (Zhongguo Zaji Tuan), and the Beijing Acrobatic Troupe (Beijing Zaji Tuan), but there are other troupes from each district of the city also well worth seeing.

Dance and Music

Beijing has two major ballet and opera companies: the Central Opera and Ballet Company (Zhongyang Geju Wuju Tuan) which uses western techniques and has a predominantly western repertoire, and the China Opera and Ballet Company (Zhongguo Geju Wuju Tuan) which combines Chinese and western styles, creating dance-dramas based on Chinese themes.

Numerous visiting song and dance troupes from the various provinces of China come to the capital. They mostly draw their repertoire from the varied cultural traditions of China's many nationalities. Though authentically costumed, the performers are often Han Chinese and the dances and songs are usually based only loosely on the original ethnic form.

At the **International Club** there is a music or dance performance of some kind most weekday evenings, and western films are shown on Saturday nights. For information, telephone 5322188.

Beijing Opera

Traditional Chinese opera is still one of the most popular forms of entertainment in Beijing. Beijing opera has a history of over 150 years and uniquely combines acting, singing, dancing and acrobatic skills with spectacular makeup and colourful costumes. The 'painted face' or *jing* character actors are highly adept in applying paint to their faces. The colours depict the whole range of human emotions of the individual character: red indicates loyalty; yellow is cunning;

Afternoon Tea

or the elderly who do not want to sit in tenements all day there is
a tea-house under the arcades. Tables and stools spill onto the
pavement: the stools are bamboo, and barely a foot high, chiefly to
assist squatting; they are very comfortable. The proprietor lurks
behind a clay oven, where a kettle hisses on a coal grate. Soot
blackens the chimney breast, the wooden ceiling, the dingy walls.
All around the tea man there are shelves and niches stacked with
earthenware teapots, none larger than a plum, and thimble-sized
tea-cups (without handles, of course) standing on ceramic trays.
A great tin caddy, bald with wear, and dented in a thousand
places, stands with them.

The tea-equipage is brought to the table. It is absurdly small—
everything is so small that were it not for the soot and the old men
and the grumpy proprietor, you could easily believe yourself
attending a dolls' tea-party in a Wendy house. The owner stomps
up with the kettle. He takes the lid from the miniature teapot,
which is stuffed to the brim with tea, and fills it with a swing of
the kettle. Four tiny cups surround the pot; he picks up the dainty
pot between his thick fingers and pours out the tea in a circle over
the cups. When the pot is drained he empties the cups onto the
tray. This is called washing the leaves, *a customary practice
which is supposed to remove the bitter edge and encourage the leaf
to expand, as well as warming the tiny cups. He refills the teapot,
and leaves you to pour the liquor into the cups, with a circular
motion, to maintain an even strength.*

The water sits briefly on the leaves, and the pot must be emptied
completely on each round: four cups are provided, even if only
two people are drinking. The first brew after the washing should
last about half a minute; subsequent brews are given a few
seconds. There is a limit to how much tea can be drunk like this
before your heart races and your mouth begins to fur. It's tea's
answer to espresso.

Jason Goodwin, The Gunpowder Gardens

blue is cruelty; white is treachery; black is ferocity. The actors' exaggerated movements form a mime which substitutes for elaborate scenery. Extravagantly stylized and symbolic, Beijing opera draws enthusiastic Chinese audiences. But despite recent campaigns to encourage it, it appeals to an ever shrinking audience. It is rare to see anyone under 50 attend (willingly) a performance of Chinese opera. Like Western classical opera, it is almost essential to grow up with it in order to savour it. Traditional Beijing operatic themes derive from Chinese history and mythology—stories such as 'The True and False Monkey King', 'Orphan of the Zhao Family', and 'The White Snake' make for an interesting evening. If you can get a synopsis of the opera before the performance you will enjoy it more. Performances can be long but there is no objection at all to leaving during an interval.

The **Liyuan (Pear Garden) Theatre** in the Qianmen Hotel presents a selection of Peking Opera excerpts geared for the foreign tourist every night during the tourist season (tel. 3016688, 3018814). The performers are members of the Beijing Opera Theatre Company, which guarantees a certain degree of authenticity. The show runs from 7.30 to 9 pm. Snacks and tea are served during the performance. There is also an interesting shop selling books, costumes, masks and other paraphernalia associated with Peking opera.

Shopping

Most tourists are anxious to buy something while in Beijing, be it an expensive piece of antique porcelain or simply a small memento of their visit to China's capital city.

Beijing has a number of interesting shops for the visitor to browse in, selling a range of attractive traditional crafts (cloisonné, jade carvings, jewellery, lacquerware, embroidery, painting, silk) which would do well as souvenirs. New shops are flourishing in the hotels and are well worth looking at—especially those at the Beijing Hotel. Department stores are better stocked, and innumerable privately owned speciality shops are opening up around the city. If you have the time or the inclination to shop around, Beijing offers plenty of scope. As a rule of thumb, buy as soon as you find what you like—you can never be sure to see the same item again.

Free markets give an interesting perspective on Beijing's blossoming consumerism, and you may also find here handicrafts not available in regular stores. Easy to visit would be the free market off Jianguomen (just round the corner from the Jianguo Hotel), or the ones in Sanlihe or at Beitaipingzhuang. Lively night markets thrive in the major shopping areas such as Wangfujing and Xidan, and sell household goods, clothes and food up to 10 pm or even later.

Although Beijing's prices are rising, there are still bargains to be had. Shoppers may discover that merchandise in tourist areas can be found in shops off the tourist route for a much lower price. Some items, however, particularly antiques and carpets, can be more expensive in China than outside (notably in Hong Kong), so if you are planning to buy something special, try and check prices at home beforehand, or in Hong Kong if you are passing through. Bargaining is not accepted in State-owned stores where prices are fixed, but, if handled tactfully, might work in smaller privately owned establishments.

Stores in Beijing are open seven days a week from 8 or 8.30 am to about 7.30 or 8 pm, and even on the few public holidays many open their doors for business.

The packing and transportation of large, heavy or breakable purchases can be arranged by the Friendship Store, whether the goods to be shipped were bought there or not, but it may be time-consuming, and shipment is expensive. Some of the major new hotels also arrange shipping.

Main Shopping Areas

There are three main shopping areas in the city—Wangfujing, near the Beijing Hotel, Qianmen and Dazhalan, south of Tiananmen Square, and Liulichang. These areas throng with jostling crowds all day long, and a browse in any of the local shops offers an insight into the life-style of the Beijing resident.

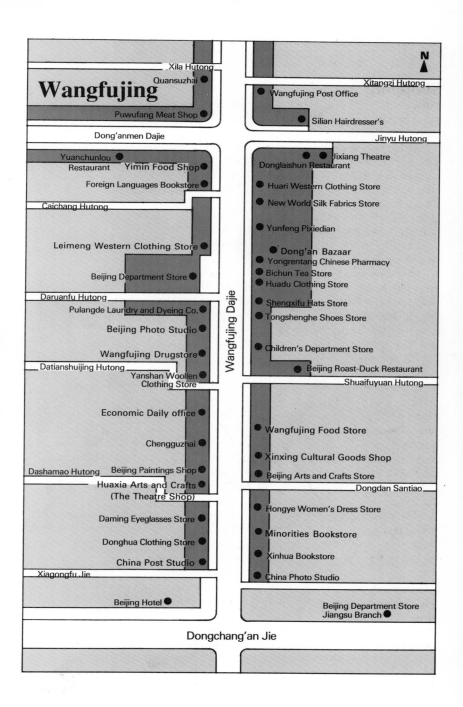

Wangfujing

N

Xila Hutong
Quansuzhai

Xitangzi Hutong

Wangfujing Post Office

Puwufang Meat Shop

Silian Hairdresser's

Dong'anmen Dajie

Jinyu Hutong

Yuanchunlou Restaurant
Yimin Food Shop

Jixiang Theatre
Donglaishun Restaurant

Foreign Languages Bookstore

Huari Western Clothing Store

New World Silk Fabrics Store

Caichang Hutong

Yunfeng Pixiedian

Leimeng Western Clothing Store

Dong'an Bazaar
Yongrentang Chinese Pharmacy
Bichun Tea Store

Beijing Department Store

Huadu Clothing Store

Daruanfu Hutong

Shengxifu Hats Store

Pulangde Laundry and Dyeing Co.

Tongshenghe Shoes Store

Beijing Photo Studio

Wangfujing Drugstore

Children's Department Store

Datianshuijing Hutong

Beijing Roast-Duck Restaurant

Yanshan Woollen Clothing Store

Shuaifuyuan Hutong

Wangfujing Dajie

Economic Daily office

Wangfujing Food Store

Chengguzhai

Xinxing Cultural Goods Shop

Dashamao Hutong
Beijing Paintings Shop

Beijing Arts and Crafts Store

Huaxia Arts and Crafts
(The Theatre Shop)

Dongdan Santiao

Daming Eyeglasses Store

Hongye Women's Dress Store

Donghua Clothing Store

Minorities Bookstore

China Post Studio

Xinhua Bookstore

Xiagongfu Jie

China Photo Studio

Beijing Hotel

Beijing Department Store
Jiangsu Branch

Dongchang'an Jie

Wangfujing

Beijing's main shopping street is Wangfujing—once called Morrison Street after the famous London *Times* correspondent who lived at number 98 at the turn of the century. During the Ming and Qing it was an area of smart residences, and, as the foreign legation grew at the end of the 19th century, Wangfujing became a prime area for buying speciality goods.

Today's shops contain a good cross-section of high-quality goods available in the city. It is crowded every day of the week and becomes almost impassable on Sundays, Beijing's main shopping day.

Visitors may spend an interesting hour or so looking around one of the main department stores in the city, the **Beijingshi Baihuo Dalou**. There is usually a crush at the counters selling electrical goods, clothing, shoes, household goods and cosmetics. There is a good selection of pure silk, and the speciality sections of the newly renovated top floor are worth a look if only to see what goods are currently in vogue in Beijing. The **Dongfeng (East Wind) Market** just across the road occupies a huge area supplying almost every basic daily need, with several small restaurants. In the last years of the Qing Dynasty the market was a maze of small shops, stalls, restaurants and theatres. At the **Dongdan Food Market**, a block east of the Beijing Hotel, fresh vegetables, meat and frozen fish are sold. Plates of pre-cut ingredients to be cooked at home are prepared for the convenience of Beijing's working wives.

One of the more interesting shops in the city is the **Beijing Arts and Crafts Store** at 200 Wangfujing, which stocks the largest selection of Chinese traditional handicrafts. Among its many items are Chinese papercuts, puppets, lacquer and cloisonné ware, embroidered linen, rattan and bamboo ware, Wuxi clay figures, colourful kites, toys, carvings, art materials and a large selection of traditional combs from Changzhou in Jiangsu Province.

Wangfujing's many speciality shops are shown on the map on page 53, and described in the shopping suggestions section (page 52).

Qianmen and Dazhalan

This general area, south of Tiananmen Square and beyond the Qianmen Gate, is particularly interesting to wander in, and its narrow streets, with charming names like 'Fresh Fish Street', 'Corridor Lane', 'Jewellery Market Street' and 'Large Gatepost Lane' reflect the flavour the area once possessed. Street sellers ply a variety of goods, from magazines and hair-rollers to pipes and suitcases, and in winter hot peanuts, chestnuts, sweet potatoes and glasses of tea. Local inns indicate the area's proximity to the railway station and many of the shoppers are from the provinces. Food shops sell local delicacies and Chinese medicine shops offer ginseng roots, fungi and deer antlers, while on the corner of Zhushikou and Qianmen one can watch the art of making bamboo steamers. Dazhalan, once known for its theatres and teashops, is still the home of the Beijing Acrobatic Troupe rehearsal house and is a busy shopping street.

Liulichang

The charming old street known as Liulichang (Glazed Tile Factory) is Beijing's best known shopping street for good quality antiques, books and paintings. It has been completely restored, and the high concentration of shops, many privately owned, make it an attractive place to wander in, even if you do not intend to buy anything.

Liulichang was established over 500 years ago in the Ming Dynasty. Initially it was the site of a large factory which made glazed tiles for the Imperial Palace. Gradually other smaller tradesmen began to cluster around, and at the beginning of the Qing, many booksellers moved there. The area became a meeting place for intellectuals and a prime shopping district for art objects, books, handicrafts and antiques.

In 1949 Liulichang still had over 170 shops, but many were quickly taken over by the State. Inevitably, much of the street was ransacked during the Cultural Revolution. Following large-scale renovation of the traditional architecture, the street reopened in 1984 under the policy that the shops should only sell old arts and crafts and cultural objects. Sadly, however, business has proved disappointing, with few Chinese able to afford the goods and tourist guides preferring to take their groups to shops where they are assured of receiving commission on items purchased.

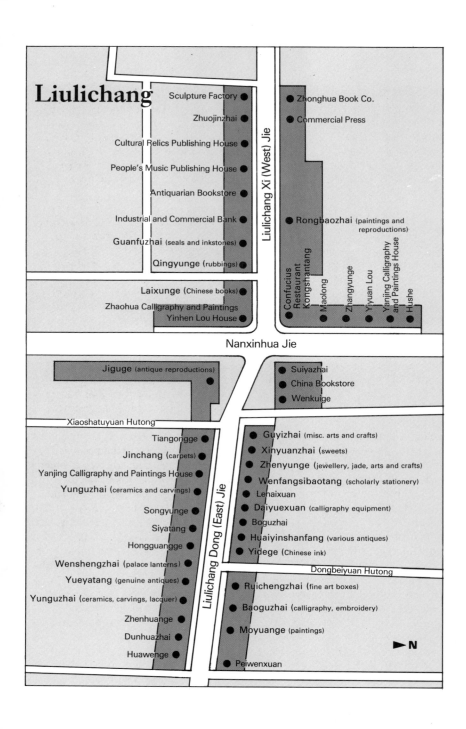

Liulichang

Sculpture Factory ●
Zhuojinzhai ●
Cultural Relics Publishing House ●
People's Music Publishing House ●
Antiquarian Bookstore ●
Industrial and Commercial Bank ●
Guanfuzhai (seals and inkstones) ●
Qingyunge (rubbings) ●

Liulichang Xi (West) Jie

● Zhonghua Book Co.
● Commercial Press

● Rongbaozhai (paintings and reproductions)

Confucius Restaurant Kongshantang
Maolong
Zhangyunge
Yiyuan Lou
Yanjing Calligraphy and Paintings House
Hushe

Laixunge (Chinese books) ●
Zhaohua Calligraphy and Paintings
Yinhen Lou House ●

● ● ● ● ● ●

Nanxinhua Jie

Jiguge (antique reproductions)
●

● Suiyazhai
● China Bookstore
● Wenkuige

Xiaoshatuyuan Hutong

Tiangongge ●
Jinchang (carpets) ●
Yanjing Calligraphy and Paintings House ●
Yunguzhai (ceramics and carvings) ●
Songyunge ●
Siyatang ●
Hongguangge ●
Wenshengzhai (palace lanterns) ●
Yueyatang (genuine antiques) ●
Yunguzhai (ceramics, carvings, lacquer) ●
Zhenhuange ●
Dunhuazhai ●
Huawenge ●

Liulichang Dong (East) Jie

● Guyizhai (misc. arts and crafts)
● Xinyuanzhai (sweets)
● Zhenyunge (jewellery, jade, arts and crafts)
● Wenfangsibaotang (scholarly stationery)
● Lehaixuan
● Daiyuexuan (calligraphy equipment)
● Boguzhai
● Huaiyinshanfang (various antiques)
● Yidege (Chinese ink)

Dongbeiyuan Hutong

● Ruichengzhai (fine art boxes)
● Baoguzhai (calligraphy, embroidery)
● Moyuange (paintings)

▶N

● Peiwenxuan

Free Markets

Visitors interested in looking at a free market could try the one located along the northeastern wall of the Temple of Heaven. Goods can include grains and pulses, peanuts, vegetables, pheasants, orchid and peony plants, dried tobacco leaves and fresh crabs in season. Sofas and chairs are in great demand and can be seen being loaded precariously across a bicycle by the happy new owner. Painters and calligraphers display their work and write auspicious marriage inscriptions on red paper upon request.

The **Guanyuan Market**, which specializes in birds and fish, is also worth a visit. It is a small, crowded spot in the northwest of the city, opposite Guanyuan Park, where Beijing's bird-lovers and goldfish-fanciers gather to admire and purchase singing birds—thrushes, mynahs, canaries, budgies and Beijing robins—carved bamboo cages, tiny porcelain seed and water bowls, and bird-food, including live grasshoppers and long fat worms. Fish-breeders defend their enamel basins of colourful fish from the crush of onlookers. Sometimes turtles, squirrels or guinea-pigs can be found there. Sunday is the best day to visit this market.

Temple Fairs

In Old Peking, religious rituals at Taoist and Buddhist temples were often accompanied by temple fairs, basically street markets where everything from food to antiques to jewellery was sold by peddlars who set up stands or simply spread their goods on a cloth on the ground. In this century, the fairs gradually shed their religious appurtenances and became purely commercial ventures where the average Beijing citizen could buy things at low prices.

Major fairs took place at five Beijing temples from three to ten or more days per month. In recent years, these fairs have been revived, although they are held only during the Spring Festival, the Chinese New Year which takes place usually in late January or early February. The fairs feature traditional toys and snacks, performances of feats of strength, ballads and opera, and general merchandise. The principle sites for these fairs are: Ritan Park, White Clouds Temple, Longtanhu Park, Temple of Confucius, Big Bell Temple, former Imperial College, and the Drum and Bell Towers. A major book fair where Chinese and a few foreign books are sold take place at the China Bookstore in Liulichang at this time as well. Watch the pages of the China Daily for announcements of the precise dates of all these fairs, or enquire at the ticket office of the venues concerned.

The Friendship Store

Friendship Stores were established to sell to foreigners export goods which were not available to local people. Nowadays some items on sale in Friendship Stores can be bought elsewhere, but the range and quality of goods is sometimes better—and the prices often higher.

The Beijing Friendship Store on Jianguomenwai Dajie has a particularly vast choice of merchandise. Shopping here is easier than in the crowded department stores, and some of the shop assistants speak English. A branch of the Bank of China is located on the second floor which will change foreign currency, travellers cheques and honour most well-known credit cards.

The ground floor (first floor Chinese-style) sells an amazing combination—meat, vegetables, canned foods, cigarettes, wine and spirits, sweets, fresh flowers, TV sets, Chinese medicine, carpets, bicycles, furniture and goldfish—principally for the consumption of the many foreign residents of Beijing. The second floor is devoted to clothing. A wide range of beautiful pure silk, Shandong silk, raw silk, brocades and cotton is well displayed. Cashmere sweaters and cardigans are reasonably priced and of very good quality. Suede and leather jackets and coats and a selection of furs are also on sale. Traditional Chinese silk padded jackets are popular, as are the comfortable black cotton shoes, while silk embroidered blouses for women come in numerous styles and soft colours. There are several tailors, but since they are usually busy with the needs of residents it is unlikely that they would be able to complete anything in a short time.

Jewellery, handicrafts, embroideries, table linen, antique and modern porcelain, ivory, jade, wood and stone carvings, coromandel screens and lacquerware are among the wealth of traditional items to choose from on the third floor.

Shopping Suggestions

Antiques

Antiques which can be exported must bear a red seal, although the red seal does not guarantee that an item is necessarily an antique worthy of the name. On the whole, the oldest pieces date from the middle to late Qing period—between 100 and 120 years old. Many pieces sold as antiques may be no more than 50 or 60 years old, but the shop assistants in the State-run stores are generally truthful about the period of any particular item, when asked. The **Yueyatang** in the Beijing Hotel is the exception. Here it is possible to purchase much older *objets d' art*, such as Ming porcelain, Tang carvings, Zhou coins, and very old paintings and calligraphy.

Most antiques for sale already have a red export seal on them—be sure to keep these on, as you may be required to show the items as well as the receipts to customs on departure. Should you buy antiques which do not have a seal, it is advisable to have one fixed. This involves a visit to the Beijing Arts Objects Clearance Office situated in the compound of the Friendship Store, open 2–5 pm on Mondays and Fridays. A small fee per piece is charged.

The best-known antique shops in Beijing are in Liulichang. **Yunguzhai** at 80 Liulichang East, is famous for its antique ceramics—vases, plates, bowls, bird-feeds and jars, bronzes and stone Buddhist carvings as well as jade and ivory carvings.

Huaxia Arts and Crafts, 293 Wangfujing, has a small but good collection of porcelain, cloisonné and other small pieces.

On Zhushikou Dajie, just opposite the Fengzeyuan Restaurant, is another shop, the **Zhenyunge,** which has antique porcelain vases, pots and dishes, lacquer boxes, cloisonné, jewellery and miscellaneous objects of interest.

Another shop of particular interest is the **Huaxia Arts and Crafts Store** at 12 Chongwenmennei Daijie. Foreign residents call this store the 'Theatre Shop' because of its collections of old Beijing opera gowns and costumes. Although not strictly an antique store, the assortment is fascinating. The first floor has sections selling embroidered linen, old fur coats, carpets and restored pieces of old Chinese furniture. Upstairs are elaborate blue kingfisher-feather hairpins, children's silver pendants, brass ink-boxes and incense burners, Buddhist rosary beads, small old pieces of embroidery and braid and odd pieces of pure kitsch of Chinese, Russian, Japanese or European origin.

The **Hongqiao Market,** as it is called, contains a bazaar consisting of nearly 50 tiny shops selling antiques and curios ranging from contemporary Chinoiserie to valuable snuff bottles, ceramics and jades. It is well frequented by resident diplomats and businessmen as well as the growing number of Chinese dealers and collecters. Here of course, the buyer must beware as well as bargain hard, but knowledgeable collectors who cultivate professional relationships with the dealers in the relaxed and timeless manner of Old Peking tend to do better here than the fly-by-night shopper.

It is not unusual for a buyer to return to a shop several days running until a satisfactory deal is reached. On the other hand, turnover can be so rapid that an item seen in the shop one morning may be gone by the afternoon, so if you see something you like, pounce on it, and at least place a deposit on it. Trading in antiques as well as collecting them, is an ancient combination of etiquette and ritual which is seeing the beginning of a revival today.

It is rumoured that Hongqiao Market will eventually be moved to the large antique trading depot at the **Jingsong Curio Market,** about three kilometres (two miles) south of Guangming lu on the Third Ring Road *(Sanhuannanlu)*.

A similar bazaar where old, but not quite antique furniture and other antiquities are sold can be found in the **Chaowai Market** north of Ritan Park near the diplomatic district.

Books

The **Foreign Languages Bookstore,** 219 Wangfujing, stocks books in a number of languages printed by Beijing's Foreign Languages Press, as well as some foreign paperbacks, guidebooks and news magazines. Art books on many aspects of China's culture and her treasures are handsomely reproduced. Translation of Chinese novels and short stories, both modern and classical, are most reasonably priced, as are dictionaries and booklets on a wide range of subjects.

The two-storey **Xinhua Bookshop** at 214 Wangfujing is the largest bookstore in Beijing. Long queues form when some new publication or popular reprint comes on sale. The books, all in Chinese, cover most subjects including languages, literature, technology, sciences and history. On the second floor are some excellent art books, and inexpensive reproductions of paintings. There is a counter selling political posters and portraits of Chinese leaders.

The **Friendship Store** has a good collection of newspapers and magazines, and the better hotels also carry a selection of foreign paperbacks, guidebooks, maps, as well as newspapers.

For the sinologist in search of old or specialized books, the best place to go is Liulichang, where there are several antiquarian bookshops (see map page 56). The best collection of art books in Liulichang is at **Zhaohua Calligraphy and Paintings House**, 4 Liulichang West.

From time to time secondhand foreign-language books of interest may be found in the **Dong'an Bazaar** further down the street.

The most pleasant place to shop for books in Beijing is Liulichang. The large traditional compound on the east side of the intersection of Liulichang Dongjie and South Xinhua Jie called Haiwang Cun (Village of the Sea King) has been taken over by the **China Bookstore** (Zongguo Shudian). The store sells mostly new Chinese books, but there is a large selection of used Chinese, Japanese and Western books in the building lining the east side of the courtyard. Here you will find books with the bookplate of the American Embassy when it was located in Nanjing in the 1940s, pre-liberation Western missionary organizations, and private collections. Prices tend to be high, but there are a few gems to be found if you are willing to get your hands dirty. Other sections of the store sell materials used in Chinese painting.

During the Chinese New Year, a week long book sale is held in the courtyard. Bound periodicals, discounted remainders and rare items for which there is insufficient space on the shelves are piled high on tables in the crisp, dry winter sun.

Several other bookstores, none of them terribly crowded, are found in the western section of Liulichang. The Classics Bookstore, Cultural Relics Publishing House Bookstore, Music Publishing House Bookstore and Chung Hwa Book

Company deal mainly in Chinese books, but many of the fine art books sold here are supplied with English notes.

Carpets

Chinese carpets of all sizes, in classical and contemporary designs in wool and silk, may be seen at the **Friendship Store** (see page 58) and at the carpet pavilion in the Round City at the entrance to Beihai Park. **Beijing Arts and Crafts**, 200 Wanfujing, also has a good collection of both Chinese and Central Asian carpets, but prices are high. Prices at **Jinchang**, in 118 Liulichang East or at the **Beijing No. 5 Carpet Factory** on Xiao Liangmaqiao Lu are marginally better than at the Friendship Store and Beijing Arts and Crafts.

Silk

The **Yuanlong Embroidery Silk Store**, near the north gate of the Tiantan, has a history of more than 100 years of handling silk and embroidery. It has the largest inventory of quality silk in Beijing and stocks various kinds of silk garments. The store's tailors will make up shirts and blouses at a reasonable price.

Furniture

Tourists interested in Chinese furniture, screens and lacquer cabinets should visit the furniture section of the **Friendship Store.** At 56 Wangfujing there is the **Restored Furniture Shop**, specializing in refinished pieces—campaign desks, grey-marble topped tables, carved chairs and vanity boxes. A similar selection is available at the **Huaxia Arts and Crafts Store** (see page 59). Plainer Ming-style chests and cupboards with attractive brass fittings, upright chairs and cabinets are to be found at the **Donghuamen Furniture Shop**, 38 Dongsinan Dajie. Most of these pieces are old and have been restored in the workshop behind the store.

A very wide selection of old furniture in various states of repair can be seen at the **Chaowai Market** to the north of Ritan Park. Be advised that the cost of shipping an item abroad is often greater than the cost of the item itself.

Furs

Apart from the **Friendship Store**, the **Jianhua Fur and Leather Store**, 182 Wangfujing, has ready-made fur, leather and suede jackets and coats, or will make them to order. Mink, fox, ermine, sheepskin, rabbit and astrakhan are usually in stock. Some of these skins are bred commercially, others have been hunted.

Jewellery

Modern and traditional styles of jewellery set with semi-precious stones are for sale in many of Beijing's tourist shops. You may find old pieces of silver in the form of pendants which were traditionally worn by children as good luck charms, small needle-holders which women wore hanging from their jacket-button, pill-boxes, or bells. Chinese skill in cutting and working jade is seen in the artistry or carved figurines, vases and medallions.

Wenfangsibaotang at 99 Liulichang East has a good selection, and **Peiwenxuan** at 37 Liulichang East is a small, charming shop selling attractive jewellery and other small trinkets.

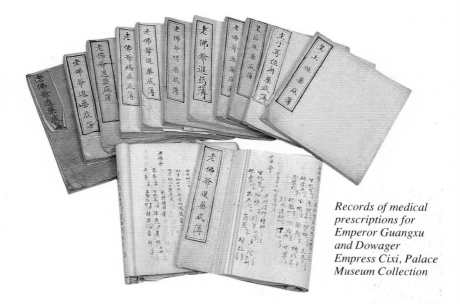

Records of medical prescriptions for Emperor Guangxu and Dowager Empress Cixi, Palace Museum Collection

Painting and Calligraphy

The **Beijing Paintings Shop**, 289 Wangfujing, has traditional Chinese paintings, watercolours and calligraphy by modern artists, stone rubbings and woodcut prints. Also in Wangfujing (at 281) is **Chengguzhai**, where paintings may be bought, and **Meishu Yongpin Bu**, at 265, which is a quality dealer in calligraphy, brushes, inks, paper, and silk-covered books. Fan paintings, embroideries, original old scroll paintings and calligraphy by some of China's master painters are found in the famous **Baoguzhai**, in picturesque premises at 63 Liulichang West.

A favourite shop is **Rongbaozhai** at 19, Liulichang West. Here reproductions of old paintings, rubbings and the works of modern painters may be found. This shop specializes in art materials, and its clients are mostly artists, amateur or professional, who lovingly feel the quality of the reams of handmade paper and discuss the merits of the squirrel-hair brush as opposed to the fox-hair brush. Decorative blocks of ink are for sale as are the various porcelain accoutrements of Chinese painting. Behind the shop are artists' workshops well worth taking a look at.

Moyuange, at 61 Liulichang East, is another good shop for paintings, and **Daiyuexuan Hubihuimodian**, at 91 Liulichang East, is a specialist dealer in the 'four essentials' of Chinese calligraphy: paper, ink, brush, inkstone.

Beijing has had an active 'underground' art scene since the late 1970s. Some of the painters associated with the democracy movement in those days formed groups, the best known of which is the Stars *(Xingxing)*. The Stars have gone abroad have had to confront the immense difficulties entailed in supporting oneself as an artist in the West. Today, a coterie of young writers and artists continues to mingle with foreign diplomats, students and journalists and peddle their art in an atmosphere reminiscent of a literary salon.

Information about these artists can most easily be obtained by contacting the cultural counsellors and attachés in the major Western embassies.

Porcelain

While wandering about the streets the visitor will find many small local shops stocking cheap, everyday porcelain and pottery, rice bowls, storage pots and small ornaments which are often quite appealing. In Qianmen Dajie are two shops selling modern porcelain. The **Hunan Pottery Products Store** (at 99) has tea sets, bowls, plates, vases and ornaments all made in Changsha, capital of Hunan Province. The other, the **Jingdezhen Porcelain Shop** (at 149/151) has products from the principal porcelain centre in China, Jingdezhen in Jiangxi Province. Pottery has been made there since the second century BC and during the Northern and Southern Dynasties (317–589) its porcelain graced the tables of the Imperial Court. Both Chinese and western dinner services are for sale in various designs, including the famous blue and white rice pattern. A 94-piece Chinese dinner service is priced from Rmb230 and a 92-piece western dinner service starts at Rmb300, depending on the pattern. Tea sets, plant holders and garden seats are among its other products.

Seals and Inkstones

Inkstones and pairs of antique and modern seals in bronze and stone adorned with delightful figures are sold at **Guanfuzhai** (Liulichang East) or at the **Yanwenzhai Seal Shop**, 261 Wangfujing. Both stores carry an impressive array of sizes and styles. The staff will arrange for your name (in Chinese characters if you like) to be engraved on the seal of your choice. Seals can also be engraved with your own Chinese name at the Dongfeng Market.

Other Speciality Shops

The **China Stamp Company**, 28 Donganmen Dajie, just off Wangfujing, sells albums of Chinese stamps and individual sets. Crowds of enthusiastic Chinese stamp collectors gather outside this shop to buy, sell or swap with each other.

For cassettes and records try the **Foreign Languages Bookstore**, 16 Donganmen Dajie, which has both western and Chinese music.

The **Beijing Chopstick Shop**, 160 Xidan Bei Dajie, has a wide selection of chopsticks, some forming sets. Strangely, this shop also specializes in walking-sticks and fans.

At the **Nationalities Friendship Store**, Nationalities Palace (Minzugong), beside the Minzu Hotel, there are handicrafts produced by some of China's minority peoples; embroideries from Yunnan, saddle-bags from Xinjiang, decorated wooden saddles from Inner Mongolia and sets of colourful minority costumes. You can even buy a nomad yurt. The **Dazhalan Hat Shop**, 9 Dazhalan, off Qianmen Dajie, has hats traditionally worn by the Tibetan, Mongol and Central Asian minorities. **Shengxifu Maodian,** 156 Wangfujing, has a wide assortment of Chinese fur hats for Beijing winters.

For silk, there is the **New World Silk Fabrics Store** (Xinshijie), at 118 Wangfujing. If you would like to buy Chinese slippers, try **Yunfeng Pixiedian**, at 122 Wangfujing, or **Tongshenhe Shoes Store** at 158 Wangfujing. (Both these stores sell China's attempts at the latest fashions as well.)

There is a large pharmacy of traditional Chinese medicine at 136 Wangfujing—**Yongrentang.**

The **Jiguge**, better known as the 'Copy Shop' at 289 Wangfujing, sells handsome reproductions of pottery tomb figures dating from the Han Dynasty (206 BC–AD 220) and later. Bronze reproductions of museum pieces, copies of wall paintings from the Thousand Buddha Caves at Dunhuang and stone rubbings are available too.

The **Nationalities Musical Instrument Shop**, 104 Qianmen Dajie, not only has Chinese traditional musical instruments such as the two stringed *erhu*, elegant *pipa*, drums and clappers, but also Central Asian long-stemmed guitars, tambourines and Tibetan horse-headed banjos. The **Hongshen Music Shop**, 231 Wangfujing, has classical Chinese and western instruments, including guitars.

Everyday Food Shopping

One of the most striking changes on the retail scene in Beijing over the last decade has been an improvement in the quality and variety of prepared food. Food stores *(shipin dian)* in every corner of the city sell cooked meats, bread and pastry, ice cream, yogurt, sweets and beverages in a bewildering variety. Many of these foods are of extremely high quality. For example, Chinese fruit jam has more fruit and less sugar than most similar products in the west. China has also enacted laws governing product freshness, and expiry dates appear on

nearly every food product. These stores also sell items produced by joint venture companies, such as Dutch-style butter cookies, Blue Ribbon beer, and very drinkable grape wine produced by joint venture wineries in northern China. The country also produces excellent hard cider. The **Palace Hotel** has a German delicatessan in one of its many basements featuring a wide range of imported sausages, salamis, cold cuts and pates, as well as mustard and bread to go along with them.

There is a small but mouth-watering selection of quality breads, cakes and pastries, imported cheeses, and cold cuts at the **Jianguo Hotel's Gourmet Corner**. For the best selection get there early, before everything is snapped up by the growing number of expatriates in the city. The **Xinqiao Hotel** has an excellent boulangerie called **Rosenbec**, which has French bread, croissants and pastries.

The **Holiday Inn Lido** also has an enticing **delicatessen** counter, as well as Beijing's first western-style supermarket. The shelves of the **Lido Market** are stocked with favourite brands of imported groceries, toiletries, cosmetics, baby food and other household items, from Hong Kong, Japan, Singapore, Europe and USA, together with some of the better Chinese brands (open 8 am–9 pm). This is the place to stock up on provisions if you are embarking on a long bus or train journey. Be aware that the prices are high. The **Friendship Store** in Wangfujing also has a number of imported everyday items, geared towards foreign tastes, but, like everywhere else in Beijing, stock does not flow smoothly, and even basic items may disappear from the shelves for months.

A number of hotel stores sell small selections of imported beers, wines and spirits, and Nescafé, even if it is not served in their own dining rooms. Prices vary considerably from hotel to hotel. The Friendship Store has a larger stock of imported wines and spirits.

Imperial Examinations

Northeast of the junction of Jianguomen and the highway, in the vicinity of the present Chinese Social Science Institute, is the site of the Ming and Qing Examination Hall (Gongyuan). Nothing is left of it now; its existence is recalled only by the streets—Gongyuan Dong Jie and Gongyuan Xi Jie—and a few *hutongs* named after it.

The system of imperial examinations, by which candidates were recruited into the ranks of the civil service, had its origins in the Han Dynasty (206 BC–AD 220). As the government of a united and increasingly less feudal China grew more complex, an established, non-hereditary, corps of officials and administrators gradually became the accepted basis of organization.

The competitive examinations tested competence in a broad range of subjects—economics, philosophy, administration—but by the Ming these had narrowed to a highly formalized syllabus based on interpretations of the Confucian classics. The increasingly orthodox responses demanded by examiners culminated in the very stylized 'eight-legged essay' (*ba gu wen*), a rigid literary form later critics condemned for its tendency to inhibit originality and creative writing.

During the Ming and Qing, examinations were held not only in the capital but also in provincial centres during the autumn. By March, thousands of hopeful candidates would be assembling for the triennial examination in Beijing. For nine days they would be confined in row upon row of tiny cells, being fed meagre meals brought in from outside and closely guarded by invigilators, to scribble away at their 'eight-legged essays' in the hopes of dazzling rewards. Success meant being received by the emperor in one of the sumptuous halls of the Imperial Palace and the privilege of joining the ruling elite. Indeed, by 1400, the examination was the only guaranteed means of entry into the imperial service. While the system was not immune to corruption—invigilators were bribed, cribs were smuggled in—it did furnish scores of talented sons of peasant families with brilliant careers and political advancement.

The ideal of the loyal scholar-official has remained a figure of awe to the Chinese to this day. Stories of their erudition and civilizing influence on warrior-emperors abound. They tell of dutiful ministers who expounded the moral precepts and historical precedents set down by ancient sages, and related them to the political issues of the day. By gentle reminders that an emperor's mandate to rule depended on 'government by righteousness,' they curbed the worst excesses of their arrogant sovereigns.

This system of competitive entry to the civil service came to be adopted by countries outside of China but, by the late 19th century, profound scholarship was no longer an adequate qualification for statesmanship. The debâcle of the Boxer Rebellion forced Empress Dowager Cixi to initiate a number of reforms. These included abolishing the imperial examinations in 1905.

History of Beijing

Beijing is both an old and a new city—old in its cultural heritage, and new as the capital of the People's Republic of China whose present leadership is determined to drag her into the 20th century.

So many of the buildings here are steeped in the history of China over the last 800 years, that it becomes rapidly obvious to any visitor how integral the city's development is to the rise and fall of dynasties, and indeed, to Chinese civilization itself.

Peking Man The story of Beijing starts a long time before recorded history. Fragments of the bones of 'Peking Man', dated to a period about 300,000–500,000 years ago, were discovered at the village of Zhoukoudian outside the present-day city (see page 135).

Capital of Conquerors During the Zhou (1027–221 BC) and subsequent dynasties, a series of large established settlements grew around Beijing. But as the area was the focus of an unsettled frontier region far from the capital—Xian—and other centres of power further south, it suffered a turbulent history.

For part of the period dominated by the Liao Kingdom (947–1125), the city was a secondary capital enjoying the pretty name (which is still used from time to time) of Yanjing, the City of Swallows. In the 12th century the 'Golden Tartars' swept down from Manchuria and wrested the city for their own, newly established, State of Jin.

When Kublai became Great Khan of the eastern part of the Mongol empire in 1260, he decided to develop Beijing as his winter capital, calling it Dadu, or Great Capital, and took up residence in a palace in what is now Beihai Park.

By the time the Venetian explorer Marco Polo reached Beijing at the end of the 13th century, it was called Khanbaliq, the City of the Khan, and was already one of the world's great metropolises. From his long detailed description of the city, it is clear that Marco Polo was utterly overwhelmed by the size and opulence of the Mongol capital.

Under the Ming

The Ming Dynasty, founded in 1368 upon the defeat of the Mongols, first established its capital in Nanjing, and on account of its relegation Dadu was renamed Beiping (Northern Peace). With the accession of the dynamic third Ming emperor, Yongle, the dynasty entered a period of vitality and expansion. He re-established Beijing as the capital in 1421, giving the city its modern name, which means Northern Capital, and which Europeans later romanized as Peking.

Much of present-day Beijing was built during the period that immediately followed. In contrast to the unplanned, sprawling cities of the south, traditional concepts of town-planning were employed, and nowhere was this more evident than in the grid layout of Beijing. The foundations of Khanbaliq were, of course, already there, but they were now extended; walls were built and moats were dug. As Beijing flourished, the city originally established by the Tartars became too small, and in 1553 a new, outer, or Chinese City, wall was built to enclose the suburbs that had burgeoned to the south.

Within the boundaries, a massive building and renovation programme created some of the most striking testimonies to Ming confidence and power. Over 200,000 workmen laboured to build the Imperial Palace between 1407 and 1420. Though the palace buildings have been restored and rebuilt many times since then, the plan remains essentially the same. The Temple of Heaven (a magnificent example of Ming architecture) and the Altar of Agriculture (which no longer exists) were erected in the Outer City. Mindful of their mortality, the early Ming emperors planned and prepared their own burial grounds in the same methodical and grandiose fashion, as can be seen at the Ming Tombs of Shisanling. Nor was the defence of the realm neglected: the Great Wall of Badaling—the section of the wall where visitors are usually taken—was also constructed during this period.

Under the Qing

For a century after Yongle, stability was maintained in the empire. But weak rulers and corrupt bureaucrats eventually fragmented the authority and drained the energies of the State. The last Ming emperor hanged himself on Prospect Hill behind the Imperial Palace in 1644, when rebels and Manchu forces were already at the city gate.

The Manchus, founders of the Qing (Pure) Dynasty that came to rule China, were descendants of those Tartars who invaded Beijing in the 12th century. This time they were to stay for 267 years.

The Qing were more interested in maintaining the existing capital and administrative systems than in making any radical changes. As they themselves became culturally assimilated (to the extent that they lost their own language), their improvements to Beijing and its environs tended to preserve the styles and techniques of the Ming period. The most interesting contributions the Qing rulers made to their adopted capital were the various summer palaces that they built outside the city.

Notable Qing rulers included Kangxi (reigned 1662–1722), Qianlong (reigned 1736–95) and the Empress Dowager, Cixi (ruled 1861–1908). During the long reigns of the former two, China enjoyed peace and prosperity. The 18th-century European ideal of the Chinese nobility as a highly cultured people dressed in gorgeous silks and much given to splendid ceremonies derived from western travellers' accounts of this land of abundance.

But the ideal was an elaborate façade; the Manchu Court had, by the 19th century, become enervated and stagnant. Clinging rigidly to ancient systems of thought and rituals, the ultra-conservative officials rejected all original ideas or innovations as seditious. Attempts by reformers to modernize China were invariably quashed.

The Coming of the Barbarians

The history of the late Qing empire is a sorry account of unsuccessful resistance to western encroachment from without, and to domestic rebellion from within. The First Opium War (1840–42) prised open China to foreign trade. In a second round of the conflict (1858–60), Beijing was actually captured by Britain and France, whose troops burned down the Summer Palaces, and whose representatives established embassies in a Legation Quarter (southeast of the Imperial Palace, in the area bounded by Dong Chang'an Jie, Chongwenmen Jie and the Inner City wall) over which the Chinese had no jurisdiction. It was this legation quarter that the men of 'The Society of the Harmonious Fists', the Boxer rebels, besieged for two months in 1900 in protest against the growing influence of the foreigners.

Piecemeal reforms, reluctantly conceded by Cixi, came too late. Her successor Puyi, who ascended the throne at the age of six, was the last emperor of China. For some years after the collapse of the Qing, he continued to live in the rear quarters of the Imperial Palace, while the front portion was turned into a museum. He finally moved from the palace in 1924.

Under the Republic

Following the 1911 Revolution, Beijing became the stage for important events in the development of modern republican China. On 4 May 1919, Tiananmen Square was the arena of an historic mass demonstration: students and patriots, in what became known as the May Fourth Movement, passionately denounced the humiliating terms for China of the newly-signed Treaty of Versailles. It was a show of solidarity that started many Chinese on the road to socialism. In 1928, when the political center of the Republic was moved to the Nationalists' power base at Nanjing, the old name of Beiping was restored to the abandoned capital. The Nationalist old guard in Taiwan continue to use that name to this day.

Emerging from its Japanese occupation between 1937 and 1945, the city had to wait another four years before regaining its paramount status. The communists entered Beijing unopposed in January 1949. On 1 October, Chairman Mao Zedong proclaimed the establishment of the People's Republic of China from the rostrum of the Gate of Heavenly Peace, and a new era for Beijing began.

Shades of Summer

HE TIME to take incense to the temple on Miao Feng Mountain had come again and it was very hot. Sellers of paper fans seemed to have emerged from somewhere all at once with boxes hanging from their arms and strings of jingling bells to attract attention hanging from the boxes.

Many things were for sale in the streets; green apricots were heaped in piles while cherries gleamed redly and brightened your eyes. Swarms of bees swooped over bowls of roses or dates and the agar jellies on porcelain plates had a milky glow. Peddlers of cookies and jellies had their wares arranged with remarkable neatness and spices of every kind and color were also set out on display.

People had changed into brighter and more colorful unpadded garments and the streets were suddenly filled with their colors, as if many rainbows had come down into them. The street cleaners worked faster, going down the road sprinkling water without a pause, but the light dust soon flew around as before and vexed people. There were longish twigs of willow in the slightly dusty air and lightly and delightfully swooping swallows as well which made people feel cheery in spite of themselves.

It was the sort of weather that really made you wonder what to do with yourself and everyone yawned great lazy yawns while feeling tired and happy too.

Processions of various kinds set out for the mountains continuously. Lines of people beating on drums and gongs, or carrying baskets on shoulder poles, or waving apricot yellow flags went by one on the heels of another, lending an unusual kind of bustle to the entire city, lending an elusive and yet familiar thrill to the people and lingering sounds and fine dust to the air. Those in the processions and those who watched them all felt a kind of excitement, devoutness, and exuberance.

The hurly-burly of this chaotic world comes from superstition; the only solace the stupid have is self-deception. These colors, these voices, the clouds filling the sky, and the dust in the streets made people energetic and gave them something to do. The mountain goers climbed mountains, the temple goers went to temples, the flower gazers looked at flowers. Those who couldn't do any of these things could still watch the processions from the sidelines and repeat the name of Buddha.

It was so hot it seemed to have roused the old capital from its spring dream. You could find amusements everywhere but everyone wondered what to do. Urged on by the heat, the flowers, grasses, fruit trees, and the joy among the people, all burgeoned together. The newly furbished green willows along the South Lake enticed harmonica-playing youngsters; boys and girls tied their boats up in the shade of the willows or floated among the lotuses. Their mouths sang love songs and they kissed each other with their eyes.

The camellias and peonies in the park sent invitations to poets and elegant gentlemen who now paced back and forth while waving their expensively decorated paper fans. They would sit in front of the red walls or under the pine trees when tired and drink several cups of clear tea, enough to draw out their idle melancholy. They'd steal a glance at the young ladies of wealthy families and at the famous "flowers" of the south and north who strolled by.

Even places which had heretofore been quiet had visitors sent to them by the warm wind and bright sun, just as the butterflies were sent. The peonies of the Ch'ung Hsiao temple, the green rushes at the T'ao Jan pavilion, the mulberry trees and rice paddies at the site of the Zoological and Botanical Gardens, all attracted the sounds of people and the shadows of their parasols. The Altar of Heaven, the Temple of Confucius, and the Lama temple had just a little bustle in the midst of their usual solemnity as well.

Students and those who like short trips went to the Western Hills, the hot springs, and the Summer Palace. They went to sightsee, to run around, to gather things, and to scribble words all over the rocks in the mountains.

Poor people also had somewhere to go: the Hu Kuo temple, the Lu Fu temple, the White Pagoda, and the Temple of Earth. All the flower markets were busier. Fresh cut flowers of every sort were arranged colorfully along the streets and a penny or so could take some beauty back home.

On the mats of the soybean milk vendors fresh pickled vegetables were arranged to look like big flowers topped with fried hot peppers. Eggs were really cheap and the soft yellow egg dumplings for sale made people's mouths water.

T'ien Ch'iao was even more fired up than usual. New mats had been hung for tea sheds, one right next to another. There were clean white tablecloths and entrancing singing girls who waved to the ancient pines above the wall at the Temple of Heaven. The sounds of drums and gongs dragged on for eight or nine hours and the brisk heat of the day made them sound especially light and sharp in a way that struck and disturbed people's hearts.

Dressing up was simple for the girls. One calico frock was all they needed to go out prettily dressed and it revealed every curve of their bodies as well.

Those who liked peace and quiet also had a place to go. You could drop a fishing line at the Chi Shui reservoir, outside the Wan Shou temple, at the kiln pits east of town, or on the marble bridge west of town. The little fishes would bump into the rushes now and then, making them move slightly. When you finished your fishing, the pigshead meat, stewed bean curd, and salted beans you ate with your baigan could make you both satiated and drunk. And afterwards, following the willow-edged bank and carrying fishing pole and little fish, you entered the city at a leisurely pace while treading on the beams of the setting sun.

There was fun, color, excitement, and noise everywhere. The first heat wave of summer was like an incantation that made every place in the city fascinating. The city paid no attention to death, paid no attention to disaster, and paid no attention to poverty. It simply put forth its powers when the time came and hypnotized a million people, and they, as if in a dream, chanted poems in praise of its beauty. It was filthy, beautiful, decadent, bustling, chaotic, idle, lovable; it was the great Peking of early summer.

Lao She, Rickshaw, (1936), translated by Jean M James

Reigns of Ming and Qing Emperors
Ming Dynasty (1368–1644)

Hongwu	1368–1398
Jianwen	1399–1402
Yongle	1403–1424
Hongxi	1425
Xuande	1426–1435
Zhengtong	1436–1449
Jingtai	1450–1456
Tianshun	1457–1464
Chenghua	1465–1487
Hongzhi	1488–1505
Zhengde	1506–1521
Jiajing	1522–1566
Longqing	1567–1572
Wanli	1573–1620

Taichang	1620
Tianqi	1621–1627
Chongzhen	1628–1644

Qing Dynasty (1644–1911)

Shunzhi	1644–1661
Kangxi	1662–1722
Yongzheng	1723–1735
Qianlong	1736–1795
Jiaqing	1796–1820
Daoguang	1821–1850
Xianfeng	1851–1861
Tongzhi	1862–1874
Guangxu	1875–1908
Xuantong	1909–1911

Modernization

Since the founding of the PRC, Beijing has become the country's political and cultural centre and has experienced many drastic changes. In the spirit of the revolution, many of the city's major monuments went the way of the city's walls and were pulled down in the late 50s. By the late 60s, Beijing was awash with the many political currents of the Cultural Revolution. At the height of this highly charged period, a trip to Tiananmen Square had become a requisite pilgrimage for thousands of zealous young Red Guards who journeyed to Beijing from the furthest reaches of China as a demonstration of their revolutionary ardour.

Political struggles, public purges and mass campaigns rent the society for a full decade before popular outrage was vented at what was to become known as the Tiananmen Incident. On 5 April 1976, 100,000 people gathered at Tiananmen Square to protest the removal of memorial wreaths which had been laid at the Monument to the People's Heroes as a tribute to the late Zhou Enlai. This public mourning for the moderate premier is now seen as a turning point in the political tide, a clear denunciation of the last years of Mao's rule and of Jiang Qing, his widow. Within six months, Mao Zedong had died, and subsequently, the Gang of Four and the political structure of the Cultural Revolution were dismantled.

With Deng Xiaoping as its new leader, China embarked on a programme of reform known as the 'Four Modernizations'—of agriculture, industry, science and technology, and national defence. The result of China's opening to the outside world has been a steady increase of cultural exchanges, joint-venture projects and direct investment from a multitude of foreign sources. International-style hotels and office high-rises now line major thoroughfares. Free markets are commonplace. The affluence of the *ge ti hu*—individual small-time entrepreneurs—is apparent as more and more families tow home refrigerators and washers, and well-heeled couples entertain themselves in an increasing number of bars and restaurants.

But with this reform, China has inevitably experienced pangs of growth. Breaking the iron rice-bowl has meant that employment is no longer guaranteed and the voices of discontent have become more vocal.

At the end of 1986 demonstrations in Beijing and other parts of China were held by university students clamouring for greater political liberalization and more rapid reform.

More recently during the spring of 1989, student protestors, encouraged by an unprecedented massive outpouring of public support, gathered for more than ten weeks in Tiananmen Square. The demontrations culminated in the death of many protestors—a trajedy all China mourned. The events of June 4th drew more attention to the conflicts and contradictions plaguing

China at the end of the 20th century than perhaps any single event in the 40-odd year history of the People's Republic.

Since 1989, many aspects of Chinese life went into recession, and what remained of the old city was being destroyed in the wake of Beijing's modernizations. Despite this, the signs of progress are now being felt. Foreign trade and tourism are beginning to return to their former levels and attempts are being made to restore historic sites damaged during the Cultural Revolution, while the city's major landmarks continue to survive as they have done for countless centuries.

Suggested Itineraries

Three full days are a basic minimum for a general introduction to Beijing, but for various reasons many visitors to the city have less time. The following lists are based on a Peking pecking order that begins with the Forbidden City.

One Day Intensive

Hire a taxi for the day. Start at about 7 am with an early morning meditation at the **Monument to the People's Heroes** in the centre of Tiananmen Square. Walk through the **Working People's Cultural Palace** and get to the **Meridian Gate** *(Wu men)*, the main entrance of the **Forbidden City**, at around 8.30 am. Spend about four hours in the Forbidden City, following the main north road to the **Palace of Heavenly Purity** and the **Hall of Mental Cultivation.** Then head east to the **Nine Dragon Screen** and north through the various exhibitions to the **Concubine's Well** and out through the **Gate of Divine Prowess**, where your taxi should be waiting for you. Have a Peking duck lunch at either Hepingmen or at the Bianyifang at 1 pm, and then spend one and a half hours at the **Temple of Heaven**, walking from north to south. Have your driver let you off at **Liulichang** for a half hour stroll around the nearby lanes and alleys, and then drive to the **Summer Palace**, arriving there by 4.30 pm, when they stop selling tickets. Stroll around the buildings and the lake until the sun begins to set, and go out for a late dinner or dine at your hotel. This is a breathless day, but feasible.

Two Days

On day one, visit the **Temple of Heaven** in the morning, then head for the **Great Wall**, where you can eat lunch. Climb the wall before or after lunch. Return to the city for a Peking duck banquet.

On day two, follow the itinerary above, minus the Temple of Heaven, or adding a visit to the **Lama Temple** on the way to the **Summer Palace**.

Three Days

On day One, begin with **Tiananmen Square** and the **Forbidden City** in the morning. Visit the **Temple of Heaven** and **Liulichang** in the afternoon.

On day two, go to the **Great Wall** and **Ming Tombs**, eating lunch along the way, or better yet, bring a picnic lunch, as the restaurants can be problematical. Eat at a Sichuan restaurant for dinner.

On day three, visit the **Museum of Chinese History** in the early morning. Explore **Beihai Park** next and have lunch at either **Fangshan Restaurant** on the north shore of the island, or eat al fresco at the snack market near **Qianhai**, across the street from the north (rear) gate of Beihai Park. After lunch spend the rest of the day in the **Summer Palace**, ideally catching the sunset there and return to the city for a late dinner.

Four days

On day one, begin with **Tiananmen Square** and the **Forbidden City** in the morning. After a late lunch, explore the **Liulichang** and the surrounding *hutongs* in the afternoon, working your way back to Tiananmen Square.

On day two, go early to the **Temple of Heaven** and watch the local devotees of the martial arts attaining longevity. Then head for the **Great Wall** and **Ming Tombs**, eating lunch along the way, or better yet, bring a picnic lunch. Eat at a Sichuan restaurant for dinner.

On day three, visit the **Museum of Chinese History** in the early morning. Explore **Beihai Park** next and have lunch at either **Fangshan Restaurant** on the north shore of the island, or eat al fresco at the snack market near **Qianhai**, across the street from the north (rear) gate of Beihai Park. After lunch stroll around **Wangfujing** and visit the shops before dinner at the nearby **Donglaishun**, featuring mutton hotpots.

On day four, visit the **Lama Temple, Confucian Temple** and **Guozijian** in the morning. Spend the last afternoon and early evening in the **Yuanmingyuan Gardens** (one hour) and **Summer Palace** *(Yiheyuan),* leaving for dinner after sunset.

Five Days

Follow the four day itinerary, and on day four, add visits to the **Beijing Zoo** (to see the pandas), **Beijing Art Museum, Big Bell Temple, White Cloud Taoist Temple, Old Observatory,** or go out of town for a half day visit to the **Tanzhesi** or **Jietaisi** in the western suburbs.

A second alternative is to visit several of the destinations mentioned above on the afternoon of the fourth day, and save the **Summer Palace** and **Yuanmingyuan Gardens** for the afternoon of the fifth day; in the morning, visit the Temple of the **Sleeping Buddha** and the **Temple of Azure Clouds** which lie about 15 minutes by car beyond the Summer Palace.

Yet another possibility on the fifth day is to make a second visit to the **Forbidden City.**

Sights in Beijing

Tiananmen Square

The enormous square facing the Gate of Heavenly Peace (Tiananmen) is the heart of modern China. During the days of the Qing empire the square did not exist—there were originally buildings on either side of a central thoroughfare leading northwards to the Imperial Palace.

Gradually cleared during the first half of the 20th century, this huge area—it covers about 40 hectares (98 acres)—has witnessed crucial developments in China's history. A number of important political demonstrations took place there during the Republic (1911–49). On 1 October 1949, Chairman Mao proclaimed the establishment of the People's Republic of China from the rostrum of the Gate of Heavenly Peace. Twenty-seven years later, the Tiananmen Incident—a riot by mobs demonstrating their support for the late premier, Zhou Enlai—heralded the end of Mao's reign and the downfall of the Gang of Four.

The **Gate of Heavenly Peace** itself is an imposing long red structure with a double roof of yellow tiles on the northern side of the square. Since 1 January 1988, tourists have been allowed to enter the gate and climb to the rostrum from which emperors handed down edicts over the centuries and Mao Zedong declared the founding of the People's Republic. Besides being steeped with historical significance, this rostrum, overlooking the Revolutionary Museum, Tiananmen, and the Great Hall of the People, provides one of the finest views of Beijing. This is the first time that this consecrated site has ever been open to the general public. However, an admission price of Rmb30 is prohibitively high for most of the Chinese population so, for most, it will remain a forbidden place.

On either side of the gate's rear portion are two parks. To the east is the **Working People's Cultural Palace**; over 550 years old, this was an imperial ancestral temple and now contains a park, a library, a gymnasium and other recreational facilities. On the western side is **Zhongshan Park**, dedicated to Dr Sun Yat-sen, the leader of the 1911 Revolution and founder of modern China.

On the eastern side of the square are two major museums, the **Museum of Chinese History** and the **Museum of the Chinese Revolution** (see page 144).

In the centre of the square is the **Monument to the People's Heroes**, an obelisk in memory of those who died for the revolution, with inscriptions by Mao Zedong and Zhou Enlai.

At the far southern end of the square (beyond Chairman Mao's Memorial Hall) is the **Qianmen** or Front Gate, a massive double gate which controlled entry to the northern section of the city.

Great Hall of the People

On the western side of the square, this monumental building, completed in 1959, houses the People's Congress. It may usually be visited on Monday, Wednesday and Friday mornings, although opening times may change when party meetings (which naturally take precedence) are scheduled. There is an entrance fee (Rmb5 at the time of writing).

The Great Hall of the People is built round a square, very much in the solid Revolutionary-Heroic mould. It is worth going inside where even if the decor is not to everyone's taste, the sheer scale of the rooms is breathtaking. From the huge reception room, the Wanren Dalitang (Ten-thousand People Assembly Hall) leads off to the west, the banquet wing to the north, and the offices of the standing committees of the national congress to the south. The Assembly Hall is over 3,000 square metres (3,600 square yards), containing more than 9,700 seats on three tiers, all installed with simultaneous interpretation equipment. Overhead, the vaulted ceiling is illuminated by 500 recessed lights radiating outwards from a gleaming red star. Some 500 guests can sit down to dinner in the banquet room, which is half the size of a football field. Gilded columns and brilliant lighting combine to produce a sumptuous if overwhelming effect. In addition to the formal public rooms, the Great Hall has 30 separate reception rooms, named after each province, provincial-level city and autonomous region of China (including one for Taiwan).

Chairman Mao's Memorial Hall

Standing behind the Monument to the People's Heroes is Chairman Mao's mausoleum. It was built in only one year by teams of volunteers and inaugurated on 9 September 1977, the first anniversary of his death, by his successor to the Communist Party leadership, Chairman Hua Guofeng. This imposing two-tiered edifice resting on a foundation of plum-coloured Huangang stone is supported by 44 granite columns and topped by a flat roof of yellow glazed tiles. It bears a striking resemblance to the Lincoln Memorial in Washington, D.C.

There are three main halls on the ground floor, one to the north, one to the south, and the Hall of Reverence in between. Entering the first, a vast reception area capable of accommodating over 600 people, the visitor will be confronted by a seated statue of Mao carved in white marble. Behind it hangs a painting of Chinese landscape.

Inside the Hall of Reverence, the embalmed body of the late chairman draped with the red flag of the Chinese Communist Party lies in a crystal coffin. The dates '1893–1976' are engraved in gold on a plaque.

The Imperial Palace

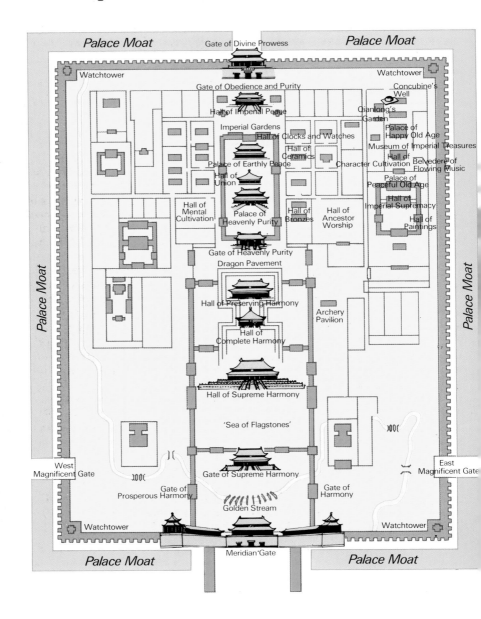

Palace Moat

Palace Moat

Gate of Divine Prowess

Watchtower

Watchtower

Concubine's Well

Gate of Obedience and Purity

Hall of Imperial Peace

Qianlong's Garden

Palace of Happy Old Age

Imperial Gardens

Hall of Clocks and Watches

Museum of Imperial Treasures

Hall of Ceramics

Hall of Character Cultivation

Belvedere of Flowing Music

Palace of Earthly Peace

Hall of Union

Palace of Peaceful Old Age

Hall of Mental Cultivation

Palace of Heavenly Purity

Hall of Bronzes

Hall of Ancestor Worship

Hall of Imperial Supremacy

Hall of Paintings

Gate of Heavenly Purity

Dragon Pavement

Hall of Preserving Harmony

Archery Pavilion

Hall of Complete Harmony

Hall of Supreme Harmony

'Sea of Flagstones'

West Magnificent Gate

East Magnificent Gate

Gate of Supreme Harmony

Gate of Prosperous Harmony

Gate of Harmony

Golden Stream

Watchtower

Watchtower

Meridian Gate

Palace Moat

Palace Moat

Leaving the mausoleum by the south hall, the visitor will see a celebrated poem by the late Mao Zedong inscribed in gold on one of the walls. The walk-through will take less than five minutes, since stopping is not allowed. Security is very strict, and handbags and cameras must be checked in before entry. There is no entrance fee.

A bustling shopping area near the exit of the hall on the south side of the building offers a wide range of new Mao memorabilia. For more valuable Mao souvenirs from the Cultural Revolution, visit the Hongqiao curios market near the north gate of the Temple of Heaven.

The Imperial Palace (Gugong)

Centre of the Chinese world for nearly 500 years, the Imperial Palace today remains the most complete and best preserved collection of ancient buildings in China. Also called the 'Purple Forbidden City' (Zijincheng) for the exclusive nature of the emperors who built and inhabited it, the Palace is a vast complex of halls, pavilions, courtyards and walls. It is within these walls that 24 emperors of two dynasties, aided by their ministers, eunuch guards, concubines and servants, acted out the drama of ruling imperial China from the early Ming in 1420 to the fall of the Qing in 1911.

Gugong, as it is known to the Chinese, is also a masterpiece of architecture. An extraordinary sense of balance is maintained between the buildings and the open spaces they surround. The scale is monumental but never oppressive; the design symmetrical but not repetitive. True to the Chinese predilection for harmony over diversity, the Palace makes use of a single style of building in an awe-inspiring combination of geomantic planning and aesthetic beauty. All the buildings are carefully laid out on a north-to-south axis, but there is no sense of rigidity to them. Like the Louvre or the Taj Mahal, the Imperial Palace is a monument that can be visited with pleasure again and again.

Originally built in 1420 by over 200,000 workmen at the direction of the third Ming emperor, Yongle, the Palace was nearly burnt to the ground in 1644 during the Manchu takeover. Rebuilt and renovated many times, it nonetheless retains the initial design set down 500 years ago.

The Palace can roughly be divided into three parts. In the foreground are four gates, each of which may look large enough to the first-time visitor to be a palace by itself. Beyond these gates, at the centre of the complex, are three principal halls, of monumental size and scope, where the emperors conducted important State ceremonies. In the rear are three lesser halls, still of notable size, and many smaller courts where the emperors and their families and attendants lived.

An Echo of the Past

W hile I was picturing the scene, an unknown voice said quietly:

'In her day there was no electricity. The attendants carried lanterns of scarlet gauze.'

I swung round startled. I had been so sure I was alone; the soft, almost feminine voice, emerging unexpectedly from the darkness and seeming like a continuation of my thoughts was disturbing.

'I beg you pardon?'

A shadowy figure, his face barely visible above a dark robe which blended indistinguishably with the night, was standing so close to me that I might have touched his hand. Perceiving he had startled me, he apologized and added:

'I saw you gazing across at the pavilions by the landing-stage. They are beautiful, are they not? But that yellowish light is out of place and garish—like so many things these days.'

'Do you mean to say you were here then?'

He laughed, or rather tittered, musically, his voice so feminine that, could I have believed it possible in Peking to encounter a woman walking alone in a solitary place at night, I should certainly have taken him for one. (The Manchu-style gowns of men and women were, even when seen in daylight, not greatly dissimilar.)

'Yes, indeed I was here then. You are a foreigner, but you speak Chinese well. Doubtless you have heard of the T'ai Chien?'

'The imperial eunuchs? Of course. But they vanished long ago.'

'Long as a young man sees things; short enough to one well into the autumn of his life. I was already middle-aged when the Revolution dispersed us. Now I am sixty.'

'Were you with them long? In the Imperial Household, I mean?'

'Not long. I was castrated in the seventh year of Kuang Hsü [1882], so I had only twenty-nine years in the Forbidden City. How quickly the time passed!'

'Castrated by your own choice?'

'Why not? It seemed a little thing to give up one pleasure for so many. My parents were poor, yet by suffering that small change I could be sure of an easy life in surroundings of beauty and magnificence; I could aspire to intimate companionship with lovely women unmarred by their fear or distrust of me. I could even hope for power and wealth of my own. With good fortune and diligence, I might grow more rich and powerful than some of the greatest officials in the empire. How could I foresee the Revolution? That was indeed a misfortune. I have sacrificed my virility and my hope of begetting children for a dream which, passing fleetingly, stopped short and can never return.'

'And so now you come here sometimes in the darkness to recapture an echo of your dream? But how do you live?'

'I manage well. I am a guide—not one of those so-called guides who live by inventing history for foreigners and by making commissions on things they purchase. I have not yet fallen to that. Discriminating Chinese gentlemen arriving from the provinces prefer to obtain their guides through the Palace Eunuchs' Mutual Prosperity Association. Often they have heard my name from their friends and are kind enough to ask specially for my services. I charge highly, for I am able to tell them many things they could scarcely learn from other sources.'

After chatting with him longer, I asked if he and his fellow eunuchs were happy in their old age.

'Happy? How could that be? We have no wives, no sons to bear us grandsons and sacrifice at our tombs. We manage to live. We are not often hungry. We dare not ask for happiness.'

John Blofeld, City of Lingering Splendour

With over 9,000 rooms spread out over 74 hectares (183 acres), the complex was indeed more like a city than a palace. The visitor entering for the first time may be surprised that each gate and hall leads to yet another, seemingly grander one, at its rear. The effect can be overwhelming and the similarity of design in buildings throughout behoves the visitor to note the special functions of each in order to gain an appreciation for the complexity of the whole. One can, with little imagination, easily understand how the emperors who ruled this Forbidden City could consider themselves at the centre of the universe.

It is often stated that there are 9,999 'rooms' in the palace, one room less than the great palace in heaven, which has a perfect 10,000 rooms. Actually, there are many fewer than 9,999 rooms in the palace, but there are nearly that number of bays (in Chinese, *jian*). A bay, in Chinese architecture, is defined as the square or rectangular space between four columns. Columns do all the work of supporting the roof in Chinese buildings; no weight is borne by the walls.

Tickets

Foreigners and 'compatriots' from Hong Kong, Macao and Taiwan can buy their tickets at either the front or back entrance to the palace, but for dramatic effect the only choice is to enter from the Meridian Gate, Wu men.

A kiosk on the right (east) flank of the gate sells a comprehensive ticket that includes all the major halls and most of the special collections for FEC18. Over the last few years, the ticket sellers have also been using hardsell techniques to get visitors to spend an additional FEC20 to rent an Acoustiguide tape of Peter Ustinoff (and other famous folks in other languages) that gives an interesting general introduction to 17 sites in the palace. In fact the ticket sellers make it seem as if renting a tape recorder is compulsory. They say, '18 *yuan* for the ticket and 20 *yuan* for the tape, a total of 38 *yuan*', which is somewhat misleading. As a rule, tour groups are not offered this service.

The Acoustiguide tour, as advertised, takes about 90 minutes. It covers only the most popular destinations in the palace, and would be best used in combination with a detailed guidebook that takes you to the other interesting corners of the palace.

Tickets are also sold in a kiosk in the parking lot at the rear (north) of the palace near the Gate of Divine Prowess. If you divide your visit to the palace into two sessions and wish to save time, you might enter from here on your return visit and go directly to the specialized collections of Chinese art that can be found in the vicinity of the Palace of Heavenly Purity in the residential quarters. But you would be sacrificing the dramatic effect of entering the palace through the awe-inspiring gates and courtyards that sealed the emperor off from the rest of the world.

The Palace Gates

By passing through the Gate of Heavenly Peace (Tiananmen) and the Upright Gate (Duanmen), one arrives at the imposing Meridian Gate (Wu men), which is the traditional entrance to the Forbidden City. The horseshoe-shape of the Meridian Gate's massive fortress walls, topped with five towers, seems to draw the visitor submissively forward through the entrance to the inner precincts. This gate was originally used for impressive functions such as reviewing victorious troops and announcing the lunar calendar. Only the emperor himself was permitted to pass through the central opening of the gate, while all others went through the sides.

Beyond this gate lies a courtyard leading to the fourth and final gate, the Gate of Supreme Harmony (Taihemen), a huge open porch supported by red lacquered pillars. One crosses a stream by one of five marble bridges, beautiful pieces in their own right that are dwarfed by the enormity of the surrounding courtyard and palace walls. Two striking bronze lions guard this entrance, the female with a cub beneath her paw, the male with a ball. They symbolize the power of the emperor and the subservience demanded by him.

The Principal Halls

The next courtyard, called the 'Sea of Flagstones' by the Chinese, was designed to accommodate 90,000 people during an imperial ceremony. In its centre stands the Hall of Supreme Harmony (Taihedian), the largest and grandest structure in the Palace. Here were held the most solemn of ceremonial occasions, such as celebration of the New Year and the emperor's birthday, or announcing the successful candidates of the imperial examinations. This hall is filled with many treasures, including bronze incense burners, musical chimes made of jade, and a nine-dragon screen behind the throne.

Behind the Hall of Supreme Harmony are the Halls of Complete Harmony (Zhonghedian) and Preserving Harmony (Baohedian). In the former, the emperor donned formal regalia before proceeding to the Hall of Supreme Harmony, or performed lesser State functions like inspecting seeds for a new planting. The Hall of Preserving Harmony was used for a time as the site for the highest level of the imperial examinations. Behind this hall, between the descending staircases, is the 'Dragon Pavement', an exquisitely carved block of marble said to weigh over 200 tons.

A Portrait of Empress Dowager Cixi

Every year, on her birthday, at an auspicious hour, the Empress Dowager would set free 10,000 caged birds. It must have been a spectacular sight to see her and her entourage in the snow-covered grounds of the Summer Palace as she opened cage after cage of exotic and brilliantly coloured birds and then prayed fervently that they would not be recaptured. By doing this, she hoped that Heaven would be good to her in her next life. She did not realize that her eunuchs were waiting on the other side of the hill to resell as many of the birds as they could catch.

Most of what is known about the Court of imperial China concerns the late 19th and early 20th centuries, for it was only then that eyewitness accounts were written. Before that, Court life was meticulously hidden from the curious eyes of outsiders, whether Chinese or foreign.

It was the Empress Dowager Cixi, effective ruler of China from 1861 to 1908, who began, in her 60s, to invite the ladies of the foreign legations to visit her at Court. Moreover, her chief Lady-in-Waiting was Der Ling, daughter of a Manchu official, who had been brought up in France. In Der Ling, Cixi found someone who could bridge Chinese and western cultures, and explain to her the many puzzling features of western ways.

In 1903, Mrs Conger, wife of the American Minister to Beijing, persuaded the Empress Dowager to allow her portrait to be painted so that it could be shown at the World Exposition of St Louis. This was a novel idea to the Chinese whose portraits were painted only after death. The American artist Katherine Carl, sister of the Commissioner of Customs in Chefoo, thus became the first foreigner since Marco Polo to stay in the Imperial Palace, and the first foreigner ever to enter the ladies' quarters. The portrait, measuring six foot by four—disappointingly small in Cixi's opinion—is now owned by the US Government and hangs in the Freer Gallery of Art in Washington. Two or three other paintings of the empress were left with her in Beijing.

Miss Carl wrote an account of her unique experience, of her impressions of her surroundings—her surprise at the 85 clocks in the Throne Room, where she painted the portrait—and of the kind and considerate treatment she received from Cixi. But it is only on reading Der Ling's recollections that we see how anxious Cixi was that Miss Carl should not become too well acquainted with Court life. Der Ling was charged to remain constantly with Miss Carl and specifically commanded not to teach the American any Chinese. Cixi was concerned that Miss Carl should not see the eunuchs punished, lest she should consider the Court officials savages.

Cixi's secretiveness pervaded all her dealings with foreigners. A special court language was used when in the presence of foreigners who understood Chinese. On one occasion, entertaining some American ladies at the palace, she invited them to see her private sleeping quarters. Unknown to them, however, the previous day had been spent in totally altering the furnishing and fitting of the bedroom so that her real taste and intimate surroundings remained unknown. Chinese subjects were also traditionally forbidden to look at members of the imperial family. Cixi was greatly surprised to learn from Miss Carl that Queen Victoria, whom she very much admired, took walks and carriage rides in public places where she could be seen by the populace at large.

The Empress Dowager was never alone, for even while sleeping she was attended by eunuchs and ladies-in-waiting who were forbidden to fall asleep. She rose early between 5.30 and 6 am. Every morning, with Emperor Guangxu, her adopted son, she would receive her ministers and generals and deal with matters of State. The rest of the day would be given over to diversions. Both Katherine Carl and Der Ling describe walks in the palace grounds, boat trips on the lake and games of dice. There were also theatrical performances of which the empress was particularly fond.

If the day was filled with diversions, the year at the Court was punctuated by festivities. Birthdays, the New Year, weddings, accessions and the seasonal festivals were celebrated with fireworks, day-long performances by eunuchs and Court troupes, presentation of gifts and extravagant banquets at which glittering gold, silver and jade tableware would be heaped with hundreds of delicacies. On these occasions the imperial family and their officials wore their grandest robes and the usual business of the Court was suspended for several days.

The Inner Court

The three rear halls, the Palace of Heavenly Purity (Qianqinggong), the Hall of Union (Jiaotaidian) and the Palace of Earthly Peace (Kunninggong), were also the site of lesser State functions. During the Ming Dynasty, emperors lived among these buildings, but later, the Qing rulers moved to smaller, less formal parts of the Palace. They nevertheless continued to use the Palace of Earthly Peace to consummate their marriages. The last emperor, Puyi, who ascended the throne as a child and formally abdicated in 1924, was allowed to use this chamber on his wedding night. However, intimidated by the colour scheme of gaudy red (the traditional colour of joy), he fled to his usual quarters.

The east and west sides of the Palace's rear section contain a dizzying succession of smaller courts where the imperial families, concubines and attendants lived, schemed for power and engaged in their many intrigues. In the far northeast corner of the complex, behind the Palace of Peaceful Old Age (Ningshougong), is the famous well down which the Pearl Concubine was cast (see page 106). Several of the eastern palaces have been converted into exhibition halls for the collections of the Palace Museum (see page 141).

Two sections in the eastern palaces are worth seeing. One is Qianlong's Garden, built for the retirement of the aging emperor (reigned 1736–95). It is a quiet, secluded rock garden with a central pavilion made of fine wood brought from the forests of Sichuan and Yunnan Provinces. One of three smaller pavilions was specially constructed for elaborate drinking games with strong Chinese liquor, a favourite pastime of the emperor.

The Belvedere of Flowing Music (Changyinge) is a three-storey theatre, the largest in the Palace, and a favourite haunt of the Empress Dowager Cixi. Magnificently carved and painted eaves set off the stage where dramas often depicted Buddhist worthies and Taoist immortals swarming all over the boards, dropping from ceilings and popping out of trap doors. The building opposite, where Cixi watched the dramas, has a rich display of silk costumes, stage properties and scripts used by the imperial troupe. There are also drawings of famous productions of the 60th birthday celebrations of Qianlong and Cixi. The latter affair is said to have continued for ten consecutive days.

Beyond the rear palaces, by the northern gate of the Palace, are the Imperial Gardens. Landscaped with cypress and pine trees that are now hundreds of years old, this is a perfect spot for a rest or a casual stroll.

Before leaving the palace, you might visit an interesting exhibition of palace architecture and construction located in the tower of the Gate of Divine Prowess. Here there are blueprints, tools, colour schemes, roof tiles and old photographs that are highly informative despite the frustrating absence of labels in any language except Chinese. Tickets for the exhibition are sold in the kiosk on the east side of the courtyard inside the gate. You reach the tower by a long incline once used by the soldiers guarding the palace.

Prospect Hill (Jingshan) or Coal Hill (Meishan)

Just north of the Imperial Palace, the site occupied by Prospect Hill was a private park reserved for the use of the emperor in the Yuan Dynasty (1279–1368). During the Ming (1368–1644), an artificial hill with five peaks was made, utilizing earth excavated when the moat of the Imperial Palace was dug. There is an old story that an emperor kept supplies of coal hidden under the hill, hence its other name, Coal Hill (Meishan). A pavilion was erected on each peak, and five bronze Buddhas given pride of place in them. Four of the statues were removed by the troops of the Allied Expeditionary Force when they came to Beijing to relieve the Siege of the Legations in 1900.

Prospect Hill was opened to the public in 1928. Designated as a park after 1949, and closed during the Cultural Revolution, it can now be visited between 6 am and 8 pm.

At the southern approach is the Gorgeous View Tower (Qiwanglou). Previously visited by emperors coming to pay their respects at an altar to Confucius, it is now an exhibition venue for displays of paintings, porcelain and calligraphy.

The best view of Beijing is to be had from the Pavilion of Everlasting Spring (Wanchunting) perched on top of the middle peak, which used to be the highest point in the city. Northwards, one can see the Drum and Bell Towers, a traditional feature of old Chinese cities. To the northwest, the two slabs of water of the Shishahai and Beihai Lake are intersected by Di'anmen Dajie. To the south, the golden roofs of the Imperial Palace can be seen stretching into the distance.

On the eastern slope there used to be an old tree (said to be cassia) from which Chongzhen, the last Ming emperor, is supposed to have hanged himself in 1644. According to one version of the incident, the emperor decamped to the hill upon hearing that rebels intent on overthrowing the dynasty had already stormed the city. He had evidently retreated in some disarray: he wore no head-dress, had only one shoe, and the sleeves of his robe were freshly stained with the blood of his consort and two princesses. The story goes that he committed suicide with his own belt. The spot was once marked by a stone tablet. Later emperors in the early Qing, passing this place to go to the Hall of Imperial Longevity behind the hill, were required to alight from their sedan-chairs and proceed past the tablet on foot, perhaps in order to show more humility when contemplating the salutary example of an unpopular predecessor.

Part of the Hall of Imperial Longevity is now the **Beijing Children's Palace**.

Reckless Pride

"I don't understand," I said. "I thought Grandmother died when Mother was a child."

"Whatever gave you that idea?" asked my aunt.

"I don't know. I just assumed . . . Mother never talks about her. Why?"

"Perhaps she was too ashamed."

"What for?"

"Perhaps you should ask her."

"No, I couldn't, not now, not after all these years. Please, Auntie, you must tell me."

Only then, when I was forty-one, did I learn that once again Grandmother had defied the inviolable mores of Chinese society.

When she failed to have a "son," even Grandfather, a "modern" man who did a wicked turkey trot, could no longer flout tradition. He announced that he would be taking a second wife. Without a word, without a tear, Grandmother packed her bags and walked out of the House of Fang forever.

When I heard this, I gave Grandmother a rousing cheer. It was exactly what I would have done. My aunt shook her head at such foolishness and said, "Do not be so hasty. How can you be certain she did not regret that decision for the rest of her life?"

The idea startled me, but I refused to consider it and, shrugging a shoulder, hastened to declare, "I would not!"

"Silly one, you are an American married to an American, living in a culture and a time where husbands and wives leave one another as indifferently as the wind changes its direction. But that was not true for my mother. She was a Chinese married to a Chinese in a culture and a time when marriage had little to do with love and everything to do with life. What kind of life could she have had without a husband, without her children, without a rightful palce? Only one of ever-deepening sorrow."

"But she was right to leave. How could she ever again have held her head high if she'd stayed?"

"You ask the wrong question. You should be asking, How could she after she left?"

Bette Bao Lord, Legacies

Beihai Park

To the west of Prospect Hill is one of the most beautiful places in Beijing. Beihai Park is open from 6 am to 8 pm (extended to 9 pm in the summer), and is a popular place for skating in the winter and boating in the warmer months. There is a jetty on the northern shore, in front of a botanical garden, from which boats can be easily hired. The extraordinarily beautiful lotus blossoms make late summer a favourite time for visitors.

A lake was first dug here during the Jin Dynasty (12th–13th century); a palace, an island—Qionghua—and pleasure gardens together created a retreat for the Court.

The retreat was refurbished three times during the Yuan Dynasty, and again overhauled in the 15th century by Emperor Yongle, the architect of Beijing. The lake was divided into two: the central and southern lakes to the south, Zhongnanhai, is now reserved for senior members of the Chinese government. Dubbed the 'new Forbidden City' by Beijing residents, **Zhongnanhai** contains the villa where Mao Zedong lived and worked. The complex is off-limits to foreigners but Chinese tours are occasionally admitted. The northern part, Beihai, is open to the public. By the south entrance to the park is the **Round City**, which contains the enormous jade bowl, with fine carvings of sea monsters round the outside, that was given to Kublai Khan in 1265. The bowl went missing for several centuries, and was functioning as a pickle vat in a monastery in the northern part of the city until the Qianlong emperor rescued it and brought it here in the 18th century. The carved inscriptions on the bowl date from this time.

The building that stands in the centre of the Round City, the **Hall of Receiving Light,** contains a large, white, jade Buddha image that resembles the statue in the Jade Buddha Temple in Shanghai. It was here that the Guangxu emperor met with the British ambassador in 1893. Former emperors would rest and change their clothing in the Round City on their way to the palaces in the western suburbs. The Round City is open to visitors from 8.30 am to 4.30 pm.

Qionghua Island

The dominant landmark on Qionghua Island also called Hortensia Island is the **White Dagoba**, a Buddhist shrine of Tibetan origin, built in 1651 in honour of the visit of the Dalai Lama to Beijing. Terraces lead down the southern slope, near the bottom of which is the White Dagoba Temple, now known as the **Temple of Everlasting Peace** (Yongansi).

Fangshan Restaurant, famous for its imperial dishes, is located among the buildings that form the **Hall of Rippling Waves** (Yilantang), a former palace, at the northern end of the island. Not far from this, to the west, is the **Pavilion for Reading Ancient Texts** (Yuegulou), which is a storehouse of 495 stone tablets, engraved with calligraphy during the Qianlong period, including samples of writing from 1,500 years ago.

The Northern Shore

Over a period of 30 years, Emperor Qianlong embellished several pavilions, halls and terraces along the northwestern shore of the lake. To commemorate his mother's 80th birthday, he had erected the **Ten-thousand Buddha Tower** (Wanfolou) at the western end of the cluster of buildings and gardens. Sadly, the little Buddhas have all been stolen, but the tower is being renovated.

Nearby, in front of the former Temple of Expounding Fortune (Chanfusi), now the site of a botanical garden, stands the **Iron Screen**, a Yuan-Dynasty wall of volcanic stone carved with strange mythical creatures. A later version, the **Nine-Dragon Screen**, made of glazed tiles in 1417, can be found further east, scaring evil spirits away not from the temple that used to stand behind, but from the Beihai Sports Ground.

Some of the old buildings around Beihai Lake have been converted to modern use; one of the most well-preserved is the **Study of Serenity** (Jingxinzhai) near the northern apex of the lake. This, deservedly called 'a garden within a garden', comprises a quiet walled enclave with a summer house, which now accommodates a literary research institute.

The Empress Dowager Cixi used to go to Beihai for picnics on the lake, and today the park continues to be a favourite with citizens enjoying a snack either from some of the small pavilions serving food, or a full meal at the Fangshan Restaurant.

The Drum and Bell Towers (Gulou and Zhonglou)

Drum and Bell Towers are a traditional feature of an old Chinese city. In Beijing they are located to the north of Prospect Hill.

The Drum Tower (Gulou) dates from the Ming period. Rising from a brick podium, the multi-eaved wooden tower is pierced on two sides by six openings. In imperial times 24 drums would beat out the night watches; now only one of them remains. The tower is being renovated, but it may be entered and climbed. Not far north of the Drum Tower is the Bell Tower (Zhonglou), a structure 33 metres (108 feet) high. The present tower was constructed of brick in 1747. The copper bell, which replaced an earlier iron bell that is still intact, rang out over the city at seven o'clock every evening until the practice was stopped in 1924.

Song Qingling's Home

Song Qingling (Soong Ching-ling), born in 1892 in Shanghai, was married to the famous Republican Sun Yat-sen and became an active political figure in her

own right after his death. Though initially aligned, through her husband, with
the Nationalist Party (Guomindang), whose leader Chiang Kai-shek married
her sister Mei-ling, she eventually split with the right wing and, after spending
several years in the Soviet Union, became a supporter of the Communists.

The Chinese accord Song Qingling enormous respect not simply because
she was Honorary Chairman of the People's Republic towards the end of her
life; she was also, in a very prominent way, a convert from the 'class enemy',
coming as she did from a powerful and wealthy Shanghai family.

Her former residence at 46 Beiheyan, near the Back Lake, (Hou hai) originally belonged to a member of the Qing royal family. Song Qingling occupied
it from 1963 to her death in 1981. It may be visited during 8.30–11.30 am and
1.30–4 pm except on Mondays and Wednesdays, and provides a relaxing
diversion from Beijing's major sights. The house is enclosed by a lovely garden
filled with pine, cypress and flowering shrubs, as well as traditional pavilions
linked by winding corridors. The Fan Pavilion (Shanting) gives a view of the
whole garden.

The living quarters have been turned into a modest museum displaying
memorabilia of the former occupant's eventful life. Song Qingling was educated
at Wesleyan College in Macon, Georgia and the bookshelves contain an impressive collection of English-language books.

The Mansion of Prince Gong (Gongwangfu)

Located at number 17 Qianhaixi Jie in the Rear Lakes (Shichahai) district,
the Mansion of Prince Gong is one of the largest and best preserved prince's
mansions in Beijing. Prince Gong was the younger brother of the Xianfeng
emperor, whose short rule lasted only ten years (1851–1861). When Xianfeng
died and the young Tongzhi emperor mounted the dragon throne at the age of
five, Prince Gong served as regent along with Xianfeng's principle concubine
and Tongzhi's mother, the notorious Empress Dowager Cixi. Prince Gong
offended Cixi when he had An Dehai, her favourite eunuch killed. Prince Gong
also represented the Chinese government in negotiations with Lord Elgin in
1860, and was a key player in Chinese politics during the troubled decades of
the late 19th century.

The mansion is divided into three sections. There is the residence itself,
with a large banquet hall now used for evening shows. The spacious garden has
several artificial hills made of heaped Lake Taihu stones, grotesquely eroded
chunks of limestone that was transported from the Yangtze delta region. Atop
one of the hills there is a pagoda that was used for gazing at the moon. There
is also a large square fishing pond with an island in its centre.

A number of literary scholars in China have suggested that Prince Gong's
mansion was the model for the mansion and garden, the Prospect Garden

(Daguanyuan) described by Cao Xueqin in *The Dream of the Red Chamber (Hongloumeng)*, the 18th century novel generally regarded as China's greatest. Indeed several details of the mansion correspond with the descriptions in the book, especially the layout of the buildings.

In the 1980s, the mansion was rescued from the clutches of the Public Security Bureau, which was using the grounds as a residence for retired officers. It is now fully restored and open to the public.

A modern Prospect Garden was built in the southwest district of the city, based closely on the novel. It was used in the filming of the television series based on the book, and is now open to the public as a park.

Xu Beihong Memorial Museum

This quiet little museum at 53 Xinjiekou Bei Dajie is one of the few public places in Beijing not crowded on a Sunday. It is dedicated to the renowned modern Chinese artist Xu Beihong, who is known internationally for his paintings of horses, and whose style has been widely imitated.

The museum was originally located at Xu Beihong's old home, but that building was demolished to make way for Beijing's subway. The present museum displays Xu's collection of oil paintings, sketches and watercolours simply but effectively. It is an enjoyable place to visit; hours are 9 am–12 noon, 1–5 pm (closed Monday).

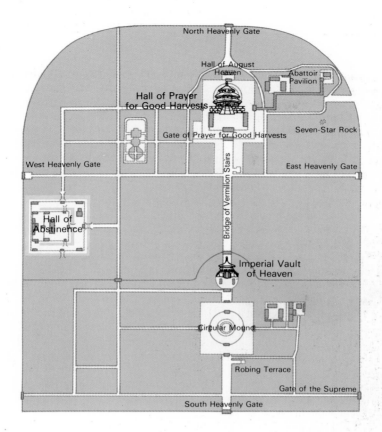

North Heavenly Gate

Hall of August Heaven

Abattoir Pavilion

Hall of Prayer for Good Harvests

Seven-Star Rock

Gate of Prayer for Good Harvests

West Heavenly Gate

East Heavenly Gate

Bridge of Vermilion Stairs

Hall of Abstinence

Imperial Vault of Heaven

Circular Mound

Robing Terrace

Gate of the Supreme

South Heavenly Gate

Southern Districts
The Temple of Heaven (Tiantan)

The Temple of Heaven has been called 'the noblest example of religious architecture in the whole of China'. Begun in 1406, in the reign of Emperor Yongle, it was completed in 1420. The huge site—twice the size of the Imperial Palace—is reached by going south along Qianmen Dajie, following a route traversed by past emperors and their entourages in splendid procession from which the commoner had to avert his eyes.

The emperors came to Tiantan at the winter solstice to offer sacrifices to Heaven— momentous occasions for which the temple's grandeur and simplicity provided a fitting background. The temple's design symbolized certain tenets of their beliefs. The altar and temple buildings are located within a wall which is half-circular to the north, and square to the south. During the Yongle period, annual sacrifices to the earth at the summer solstice were also performed here; the outline of the enclosure represented the imagined shapes of heaven (curved)

and earth (square). Note that the roof tiles of the Hall of Prayer for Good
Harvests (see below) are a deep blue, the colour of the sky. Moreover, each
of the main structures in the temple has three tiers, making a total of nine, a
number in Chinese cosmology representing Heaven. A separate Altar to the
Earth (Ditan) was later constructed to the north of the city.

From the entrance at West Heavenly Gate, an avenue leads to the Hall of
Abstinence (Zhaigong). For three days before the rites began, the emperor would
have forsworn meat and wine, and the last day of his fast would be spent here.
For his safety, the hall was enclosed by a moat.

From there visitors can walk up to the Circular Mound (Yuanqiu), an open
altar set on three round marble terraces, built in 1530. The emperor used to come
here to commune with Heaven and, interestingly, there is a curious acoustical
effect to be heard from the centre of the Circular Mound.

Next to the Mound is the Imperial Vault of Heaven (Huangqiongyu),
a wooden structure roofed with blue tiles and built entirely of wood in 1530.
Tablets used in ceremonies held on the Mound were stored here. The Imperial Vault is surrounded by a round wall, popularly known as the Echo or
Whispering Wall, because of its remarkable acoustics. If the round courtyard
is relatively quiet—something it has not been in several years due to the rising
tide of domestic tourism—two people standing at any point along the wall with
their heads at approximately the same distance off the ground can hear each
other talking.

A second acoustical phenomenon is the 'echo stones', which refer to the first
three rectangular stones at the foot of the staircase that leads up to the Imperial
Vault. If you stand on the first stone at the foot of the stairs and clap your hands
once, you will hear one echo. If you clap once on the second stone, you will
hear two echos. And a single clap from the third stone will produce three echos.
Again, this 'works' only if the courtyard is quiet enough for the vibrations to
resonate in peace.

Leaving the Imperial Vault, there is a fine walk along a raised approach
called the Bridge of Vermilion Stairs to the main building of the park, the
magnificent Hall of Prayer for Good Harvests. This round wooden hall is
surmounted by a triple roof covered in blue tiles and crowned with a gilded
ball. The walls are resplendently painted in rich colours—red, blue, gold and
green. It stands on three marble terraces.

The original Hall of Prayer for Good Harvest was built in 1420, but burned
down in 1889 and was later reconstructed. At the time, there were no trees in
China tall enough to supply the wood for the four tall columns, and thus these
pillars, representing the four seasons and four directions, were imported from
Oregon in the USA by the American lumber dealer, Robert Dollar—a fact that
appears in no guidebook published in China since 1949. This showpiece of

architectural ingenuity, 39 metres (125 feet) high and supported by 28 wooden pillars, stands without the aid of nails.

The Hall was last used in 1914 by Yuan Shikai, then President of the infant Republic, who had imperial ambitions.

Two rectangular buildings stand in the courtyard before the Hall. The one on the west is a large comprehensive gift shop, while the one on the east now contains a display of the musical instruments, both authentic and in the form of reproductions, used in the imperial rituals.

Both the Altar and the Hall of Prayer are circular structures enclosed by square courtyards, a design symbolizing the journey from earth to heaven as the supplicant approached the place of worship.

Behind the Hall of Prayer for Good Harvests is the Hall of August Heaven (Huangqiandian), where many of the objects used in the ceremonies are now exhibited.

None of Beijing's other three altars can compare with the Temple of Heaven, but potentially the finest is the **Altar of the Earth** (Ditan), built in 1530, and set in a wooded park in the northeast of the city. The Hall of Abstinence there has already been renovated. Some of the buildings of the **Altar of the Sun** (Ritan), built in 1531, as well as the altar itself, still exist in a pleasant park near the Friendship Store. The **Altar of the Moon** (Yuetan) on the opposite side of the city, also built in 1531, is now the site of a television tower.

The Source of Law Temple (Fayuansi)

Situated in Fayuansi Qian Jie off Niu Jie in the Xuanwumen district, this temple is in the southwest quarter of the city. It was built by the Tang emperor Taizong in AD 654 in memory of troops killed in a battle with the Koreans and has been restored many times since. Two pagodas used to stand beside the temple, but they were destroyed by fire in the middle of the Tang. It was at Fayuansi that the Song Minister Xie Dieshan, brought under guard by Yuan troops to Beijing, chose to starve himself to death rather than submit to the Mongols.

The Fayuansi comprises six courtyards planted with lilac trees. In the past, the temple was obliged to lay on a series of vegetarian banquets every spring for local dignitaries, for it is an age-old Chinese custom to spend a convivial evening wining and dining with crowds of friends on the pretext of admiring the season's new blooms.

The present occupants belong to the Chinese Buddhist Theoretical Institute, and the temple buildings now provide accommodation and classrooms for a number of novice monks. Some fine statues in bronze and wood, as well as manuscripts and stone engravings, are on display.

The temple is open 8.30 am–12 noon and 1.30–4 pm. It is closed on Wednesdays.

The Concubine in the Well

If the walls of the Forbidden City enclosed a dazzling Court presided over by enlightened emperors, they also—down the centuries—hid the innumerable plots, intrigues and betrayals that were played out in the struggles for power. It is said that the Forbidden City is a graveyard of souls; within its tortuous precincts, inexplicable deaths and suspected murders were almost a familiar feature of Court life. There were always, at one time or another, the conflicting interests of pretenders, concubines, eunuchs and ministers to be resolved, especially when questions of succession were involved, or when weak emperors—either because of extreme youth or sheer incompetence—could be manipulated by self-seeking regents and corrupt officials.

The method of exterminating rivals by secret murder was employed with particular frequency, even finesse, by the Manchu Empress Dowager Cixi. This venal and selfish woman, who was supreme ruler of China for nearly half a century (from 1861 to 1908), has been regarded with such horror and fascination that, in the popular mind, the facts of her life have become blurred by legend.

As a young woman, Cixi entered the palace as a low-ranking concubine to Emperor Xianfeng (reigned 1851–61). On producing a son, she was promoted to Concubine of the First Grade, and skilfully charmed the emperor until she held him in thrall. On the emperor's death, she continued her scheming to eliminate her rivals and eventually achieved such considerable power that she was in a position to have herself and her sister, Empress Ci'an declared as regents during the minority of Emperor Tongzhi, her five year-old son. (Even Ci'an was eventually disposed of, by poison it is said, in 1881.) When Tongzhi came of age, Cixi, instead of relinquishing her power, thwarted his attempts to be with his wife and encouraged him in a life of debauchery, which no doubt hastened his death at the age of 18, leaving no heir.

In flagrant defiance of succession laws, Cixi then contrived to put her infant nephew, whom she adopted, on the throne as Emperor Guangxu. She ruled in his name, 'behind a silk screen', until he reached maturity and she ostensibly retired to the Summer Palace in 1889. Nevertheless she continued to meddle in Court affairs. In 1898, in the wake of China's humiliating defeat in the Sino-Japanese War, Guangxu launched the abortive reform movement that was to cost him his freedom. He was kept in semi-captivity by Cixi, who emerged from retirement to assume supreme control of the government once more.

At the height of the chaos following the anti-foreign Boxer Rebellion, the Empress Dowager was to commit one of her most ruthless murders. The date was 15 August 1900. At the time all of Beijing was in alarm as the Allied troops approached to relieve the besieged legation quarter of foreigners. In the Forbidden City, the Empress Dowager made ready to flee to the western city of Xi'an. Donning the dark blue clothes of a peasant woman, Cixi cut her long lacquered nails and dressed her hair in Chinese style. She summoned the young emperor to prepare by torchlight for their immediate departure in three horse-drawn carts.

At the last moment, the Pearl Concubine (Zhenfei), who was the emperor's favourite, appeared before Cixi and audaciously proposed that either the emperor be allowed to stay in Beijing or that she be allowed to accompany him to the west. Like the Empress Dowager, who had been a concubine herself, this spirited young woman was not given to showing respect or submission to her superiors. She had frequently interfered with Cixi's plans by giving the emperor contrary advice. Now, it must have appeared to the Empress Dowager, the Pearl Concubine had finally over-reached herself.

According to one account, Cixi lost no time in giving orders to her trusted eunuchs, who swiftly wrapped the concubine in a carpet and carried her off, over the young emperor's objections, to the rear of the palace, where they threw her down a well. Her body was recovered a year later and temporarily buried in a field in the city's western suburbs. Later she was laid to rest in the concubines' grave, near Emperor Guangxu's mausoleum, in the Western Qing Tombs.

The well is still there, inconspicuously marked by a small Chinese plaque, in a tiny courtyard in the northeastern corner of the Imperial Palace, by the Palace of Peaceful Old Age. A few Chinese tourists are usually clustered around it, trying to figure out how the eunuchs could have forced someone down so small an opening.

The final mystery surrounding Cixi was the strange coincidence of her death with that of Emperor Guangxu's. It is alleged that Cixi, adamant that the emperor should not outlive her, gave orders from her deathbed for him to be poisoned, but that is just one more sinister intrigue that will never be proved.

ial dragon robe and
dered shoes, late Qing Dynasty,
Museum collection

Niu Jie Mosque (Niu Jie Qingzhensi)

Of the 80-odd mosques in Beijing, this one, right in the centre of the city's Moslem district, is the largest and oldest—it was built in AD 996 by Nazruddin, son of an Arab priest. The mosque is open daily from 4 am to 7 pm.

The exterior of the mosque gives very little hint that it is other than a temple, but inside the gate there is a hexagonal Tower for Viewing the Moon, serving an Islamic purpose. This structure enables the imam to determine the beginning and end of Ramadan according to sightings of the moon. Grouped round courtyards behind the tower are the main prayer hall with its entrance facing west (towards Mecca), a stele pavilion, the minaret from which the muezzin calls believers to prayer, a bath-house and some classrooms. The prayer hall is decorated in bright red and gold, with a section reserved for women behind a screen.

Islam was introduced to China in the Tang Dynasty (618–907) and today the religion is embraced by several racial minorities in the country as well as the Hui, a more widespread community of Moslems distinguishable from the ethnic Chinese only by the faith they profess.

White Clouds Taoist Monastery (Baiyunguan)

Located approximately one kilometre (2/3 of a mile) south of the Yanjing Hotel on Binhe lu off Baiyun lu, the White Clouds Taoist Monastery is one of the most important Taoist temples in China. The first Taoist monastery was built on this spot in the eighth century, but the present incarnation is the result of two over-hauls that took place in 1956 and 1981.

The most famous inhabitant of the monastery was the Yuan-dynasty monk, Qiu Chuji, to whom one of the halls is dedicated. The period during which Qiu rebuilt the monastery, around 1230, is regarded as its golden age.

Like all other religious institutions in China, the White Clouds Monastery was hard hit during the Cultural Revolution, but now 100 monks, including young adepts, live on the premises, all of whom belong to the *chuanzhen* sect of Taoism. The monastery is the headquarters of the China Taoist Association, and thus is actively involved in 'foreign affairs'. The monastery performs a number of traditional Taoist ceremonies for a fee, and is crowded with believers and curiosity seekers on the two dozen Taoist holy days every year. In the old days, a major three-day ritual including horse races in the street took place here during the first lunar month, but this practice has long ceased.

The monastery is laid out on three parallel axes, with the most important structures on the central axis. There is a peaceful courtyard containing an ordination platform that resembles a miniature outdoor stage in the rear section of the western axis. Immediately inside the main gate, there is a stone-lined pond spanned by a bridge with an oversize Chinese coin hanging from it. Good luck is accorded to whoever can hit the giant coin with a coin of the realm. All the profits go to the monastery.

The White Clouds Monastery is closed Monday. There is a modest admission charge.

Prospect Garden (Daguanyuan)

In 1986 a new park, complete with pavilions, ponds, miniature hillocks and piped music, was opened to the public. Located in the southwest corner of the city, this pleasure ground has been built in imitation of the garden meticulously described in the great Chinese classic, *The Dream of the Red Chamber* (Honglou Meng) by Cao Xueqin. As recounted in the novel, the name 'Daguanyuan' was chosen by Imperial Concubine Yuanchun on a visitation. She wrote:

> *Embracing hills and streams, with skill they wrought*
> *Their work at last is to perfection brought.*
> *Earth's fairest prospects all are here installed,*
> *So 'Prospect Garden' let its name be called!*

(From *The Story of the Stone*, translated by David Hawkes)

Although somewhat lacking in authenticity, Daguanyuan is a pleasant park which is already drawing crowds of local visitors. It recently served as the setting for a major television series based on the novel that enjoyed great success in China as well as Hong Kong and other overseas communities. Perhaps someday it will be dubbed in English.

Western Districts
The Temple of the White Dagoba (Baitasi)

The 48-metre (150 feet)-high Yuan-Dynasty dagoba, off Fuchengmennei Dajie, dominates the city's northwestern skyline. It is to the west of the White Dagoba in Beihai Park.

Even at the time it was completed in 1279, under the supervision of a famous Nepalese architect, it was considered one of the gems of the Mongols' new capital. A large monastery was established here by Kublai Khan which was later destroyed, but rebuilt and renamed Miaoying Temple during the Ming Dynasty. A beautiful filigree copper canopy, hung with bells, tops the dagoba.

The temple suffered damage during the Cultural Revolution and in the 1976 earthquake, but it has now been restored. The four existing halls date from the Qing and contain Yuan and Ming Buddhist statues and Tibetan *tankas*. During the restoration Buddhist scriptures and other relics dating from the Qianlong period were discovered and are now on display.

The Five Pagoda Temple (Wutasi)

In the reign of Ming emperor Yongle (reigned 1403–24) a temple, to be named
Zhenjuesi (Temple of the True Awakening), was ordered to be built on this site.
It was to house a model of the famous ancient Indian Buddhist temple in
Bodhgaya that was presented by an Indian monk to the Court. In 1473, in the
reign of Emperor Chenghua, a building with five pagodas, based on the
Bodhgaya model, was finally constructed here. Ransacked by English and
French troops towards the end of the Qing, the temple never recovered its
former glory. The five-pagoda building still stands, however, and its stone bas-
relief carvings of figures and flowers, which are beautiful and varied, have been
preserved. The Five Pagoda Temple is located one kilometre (half-a-mile) north
of the Beijing Zoo in the Haidian district, off Baishiqiao Lu.

The Big Bell Temple (Dazhongsi)

This charming small temple near the Friendship Hotel on the West Ring Road
(Beihuan Xi Lu) in the northwest corner of the city was built in 1733. In 1743 a
huge bell was brought here, and the temple's name was changed to Dazhongsi.
The giant bronze bell is believed to have been cast in the Ming Dynasty, during
the reign of Yongle, and is by this reckoning more than 550 years old. Over
seven metres (nearly 23 feet) high and weighing 46 tons, it is inscribed with
Buddhist scriptures in Chinese characters and is regarded as one of China's
national treasures.

The bell is housed in a tower at the back of the temple, in an inner courtyard.
Also displayed in the courtyard are some 30 bronze bells from various periods,
showing the high degree of skill and workmanship that had been achieved.
Many stone steles and statuary can be seen here, too. One can go right to the top
of the Bell Tower by climbing a spiral staircase.

Beijing Zoo (Beijing Dongwuyuan)

The zoo is located in the northwest part of the city. Visitors usually go straight
to see the giant pandas to the left of the main entrance, but there are many other
interesting animals to be seen—among them tigers from the northeast, yaks from
Tibet, enormous sea-turtles from China's seas , and lesser-pandas from Sichuan.

The Beijing Zoo has an interesting history, dating back to the 17th century,
when it was a garden belonging to one of the sons of Shunzhi, the first emperor
of the Qing dynasty. In 1747, the Qianlong emperor refurbished it as a park, and
carried out many other major repairs on the imperial properties throughout
Beijing and in the summer palaces in the western suburbs, in honour of his
mother's 60th birthday.

In 1901, the Empress Dowager did another major rebuilding job, and used it to house a collection of animals given to her as a gift by a Chinese minister who had acquired them at great cost during a trip to Germany. By the 1930s, most of them had died and were stuffed and put on display in a museum on the grounds. The zoo is open from 7.30 am to 6 pm.

Former Residence of Mei Lanfang

Mei Lanfang (1894–1961) is regarded as one of the Four Great Female Impersonators in the history of the Peking Opera, an art form poorly understood and not widely appreciated outside of China and Chinese communities abroad. Mei's skill enabled him to perform women's roles more convincingly than any woman, so say the experts.

The courtyard house Mei lived in during his last days is open to the public as a shrine at number 9, Huguosi jie in the Western District. His studio contains many of Mei's personal possessions, and there are videotapes of the great diva's performances to watch.

But like the other 'former residences' open to the public in Beijing, Mei's home can be enjoyed for its architecture alone.

Northern Districts
Western Yellow Temple (Xihuangci)

Located approximately two kilometres (one-and-a-half miles) north of the Ring Road on Huangsilu in the Andingmenwai district, the Western Yellow Temple is one of the finest monuments of Lamaism in Beijing. It is all that remains of two temples, the Eastern and Western Yellow Temples, that were demolished in 1958 during the period of the Great Leap Forward.

During the Ming Dynasty, two Buddhist temples stood in this vicinity, but both were destroyed by Li Zicheng when he invaded Beijing in 1643 and brought about the fall of that dynasty. In 1651, the first Qing emperor rebuilt the eastern temple to provide temporary accommodation for the Dalai Lama's visit to Beijing, and one year later the western temple was built to house the Dalai Lama's retinue.

As one of many Lamist temples in Beijing, this was the venue for the annual performance of the 'devil dances' that took place on the 13th and 15th days of the first lunar month in the new year. (They are still performed today in the nearby Lama Temple.) By the early 20th century, most of the buildings had fallen into disrepair.

The surviving 'marble pagoda' dates from 1781, when the Qianlong emperor had it built to commemorate the death of a Panchen Lama who died of smallpox

Chengde: Imperial Resort

Chengde lies 354 kilometres (220 miles) northeast of Beijing and is the site of Jehol, or 'Warm River', the beautiful 18th-century resort of the Manchu emperors of the Qing Dynasty. From 1681 the emperors used to escape the scorching Beijing summer and travel north, over the Great Wall, to the cool hunting grounds of Jehol.

The journey, which took the imperial household at least two weeks, takes today's tourists, travelling by train from Beijing, a mere five and a half hours.

The wooded river basin in which Chengde lies is surrounded by pleated hills, punctuated at intervals by strange rock formations. Emperor Kangxi created the palace, lakes and parks to blend in with the natural beauty of the site. The palace itself is an appropriately simple building, constructed of *nanmu*, a hard aromatic wood. The audience chamber, the Modest and Responsible Hall, is connected to the other chambers by *lang*, or covered walkways, that wind around the courtyards which are themselves shaded by ancient pines.

Through the palace it is only a few minutes walk to the park and lakes. Emperor Kangxi decreed that 36 beauty spots were to be created in the park. His grandson Qianlong then doubled the number. As you wander beside the lake, there are carefully placed brightly coloured bridges which are designed to arouse your curiosity and lure you to one of the beauty spots—a pavilion such as the Hall of Mists and Rain, or the Golden Hill Pavilion.

Outside the palace grounds, Emperor Qianlong built eight magnificent temples, seven of which still remain. The eight, which was built of bronze, was removed by the Japanese during the war. The first to be built was the Temple of Universal Peace (Puningsi), in 1775. This was a period in Chinese history of massive annexations, including Tibet and what is now Xinjiang. To integrate and, in some cases, to placate his new subjects, the emperor modelled the temples on their religion and culture. For this reason the Putuozongshengmiao is a copy of the Potala at Lhasa in Tibet.

Jehol lost favour with the Qing Court after the unfortunate—and ominous— accident to Emperor Jiaqing, who was struck dead by lightning there. The summer palace and temples now form part of a public park.

when he was visiting the capital. The octagonal stupa, supposedly containing the clothing of the deceased lama, is carved with scenes from the life of the Buddha. In 1990, the carvings were defaced by the foreign troops during the Boxer Uprising. But after being repaired they were defaced once again by Chinese troops.

The Yellow Temple bears comparison with the Five Pagoda Temple, which stands a few minutes north of the Beijing Zoo.

Eastern Districts
The Lama Temple (Yonghegong)

The Lama Temple or the Palace of Harmony and Peace was built in 1694. It can be found on Dongsi Bei Dajie in the northeast of Beijing.

The prince who eventually became Emperor Yongzheng (reigned 1723–35) lived in this palace. Chinese tradition requires an emperor's former residence to be used as a temple upon his accession to the throne, so the palace was duly converted to serve a religious function.

Under the Qianlong emperor it became a centre of learning for the Yellow Hat sect of Tibetan Lamaism with considerable religious and political sway. As the residence of a 'Living Buddha' it had, at one time, a community of 1,500 Tibetan, Mongol and Chinese lamas. Today there are some 70 Mongolian lamas tending the temple.

The complex is arranged as a series of five halls and courtyards leading from a long pretty garden at the entrance. Passing drum and bell towers and two stele pavilions to left and right, the visitor reaches the Hall of the Celestial Guardians (Tianwangdian). Inside is a statue of Maitreya, the Buddha to Come, flanked on four sides by the Celestial Guardians of the East, South, West and North. Also revered is a statue of Wei Tuo, whose meritorious deeds, it is said, included the safeguarding of a bone of Buddha's.

Coming out of Tianwangdian, the visitor will come upon a large copper *ding* (ancient cauldron), cast in 1747. It has been claimed that there are only two examples of this type of *ding* in the whole of China.

The Great Stele Pavilion comes next: it contains a square stele inscribed in four languages (Han, Manchu, Mongolian and Tibetan) describing the philosophy of Lamaism.

The main hall, the Hall of Harmony and Peace, from which the temple takes its name, contains three statues of Buddha—past, present and future—and at their side figures of the 18 *louhan* (disciples who had vowed always to remain on earth to spread the teachings of Buddha).

To the north of the Hall of Eternal Blessing (Yongyoudian), is the Hall of the Wheel of the Law (Falundian). Its roof supports five small pavilions of Zongkapa (1417–78), who founded the Yellow Hat Sect of Tibetan Buddhism. Against the walls a collection of several hundred Tibetan scriptures is stored.

The last hall, the three-storeyed Pavilion of Ten-thousand Fortunes (Wanfuge) contains a unique example of Chinese carpentry—a massive statue of Maitreya. Standing over 23 metres (75 feet) high, his head reaches the third floor. The statue is supposed to have been carved out of a single white sandalwood tree, transported all the way from Tibet in the mid-18th century.

The low galleries lining both sides of some of the courtyards were originally study halls for the lamas and now contain a fine collection of Tibetan bronzes and *tanka* paintings.

The temple is open from 9 am to 5 pm, and closed on Mondays.

The Old Observatory (Guanxiangtai)

Kublai Khan established an observatory at the southeastern corner of his city and it is still there today. Functioning as part of the more modern Beijing Observatory and Planetarium (which is right at the other end of the city, opposite the Beijing Zoo in the northwest), the Old Observatory is now a museum with a small collection of superb Ming and Qing astronomical instruments.

Of the instruments that were made from the 15th century onwards only 15 pieces remain, including several made by Jesuit fathers—notably Adam Schall and Ferdinand Verbiest—in the 17th century. When these missionaries came to China they proved themselves to be such skillful astronomers that they were put in charge of the observatory.

These instruments were taken to Germany in 1900, as spoils of war after the Allied forces had subdued the Boxer Rebellion, but were returned to China in 1919. Eight of them are displayed on the Observatory terrace here atop one of the few remaining sections of the old city wall (the other seven were moved to the Nanjing Observatory in 1931). They include three armillary spheres, a quadrant, a sextant, a celestial globe, a horizon circle and a quadrant altazimuth.

The observatory may be visited during 9–11.30 am and 1–4.30 pm but is closed on Fridays.

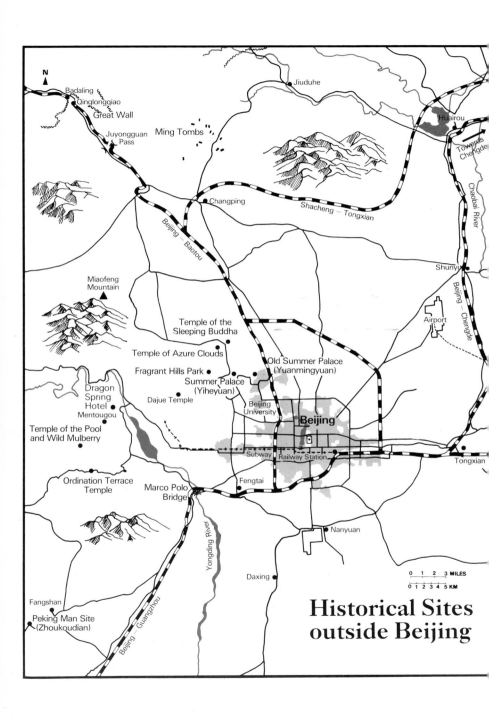

N

Jiuduhe

Badaling
Qinglongqiao
Great Wall
Juyongguan
Pass
Ming Tombs

Huairou

Towards
Chengde

Changping

Shacheng – Tongxian

Beijing – Baotou

Chaobai River

Shunyi

Beijing – Chengde

Miaofeng
Mountain

Airport

Temple of the
Sleeping Buddha

Temple of Azure Clouds

Old Summer Palace
(Yuanmingyuan)

Fragrant Hills Park

Summer Palace
(Yiheyuan)

Dragon
Spring
Hotel
Mentougou

Dajue Temple

Beijing
University

Beijing

Temple of the Pool
and Wild Mulberry

Subway

Railway Station

Tongxian

Ordination Terrace
Temple

Marco Polo
Bridge

Fengtai

Yongding River

Nanyuan

Daxing

Fangshan

Peking Man Site
(Zhoukoudian)

Beijing – Guangzhou

0 1 2 3 MILES

0 1 2 3 4 5 KM

Historical Sites
outside Beijing

Sights Outside Beijing

The Northwest

The Summer Palace (Yiheyuan)

In order to avoid the intense heat of the summer, the imperial Court used to leave the Forbidden City and stay in a specially built resort about 11 kilometres (seven miles) northwest of Beijing. Known in the west as the Summer Palace and in China as Yiheyuan—the Garden for Cultivating Harmony—the resort encompasses Longevity Hill (Wanshoushan) and a series of palaces, pavilions, terraces and covered walks strung out along the northern shore of Kunming Lake. Indeed the Summer Palace is three-quarters covered by water and Kunming Lake, whose shape and size have been altered many times by successive landscape architects, is central to the overall design of the park. The indefatigable Emperor Qianlong, for one, reconstructed it to resemble the West Lake in Hangzhou in 1751, the year of his mother's 60th birthday (Longevity Hill was named for her).

The Old Summer Palace know as Yuanmingyuan (see page 122) was ravaged by Anglo-French troops in 1860. In 1888 the Empress Dowager Cixi diverted funds allocated for improving the navy to the Summer Palace's renovation at a new site. She gave it its present name, Yiheyuan, and retired to its peaceful environs in 1889. Following further destruction in 1900, the Summer Palace was again restored at great expense.

The Summer Palace today is a delightful park, informal and less imposing than the Imperial Palace. Much has been restored and it is in a fine state of preservation.

Imperial Residences

Directly opposite the East Palace Gate (Donggongmen), across a large court-yard, is the Hall of Benevolent Longevity (Renshoudian) where Cixi and her nephew, the nominal emperor Guangxu, gave audience to their ministers. Behind the courtyard were the private apartments of the imperial household, the Hall of Jade Ripples (Yulantang). This residence was made even more private when the Empress Dowager had a wall erected on its lake side. Here Guangxu was for ten years her prisoner, having flouted her authority by giving his support to an ill-fated reform movement in 1898. With him safely under guard (but officially 'chronically ill'), she emerged from 'retirement' to assume control of the government once more.

Cixi's own quarters were in the Hall of Happy Longevity (Leshoutang), with Longevity Hill behind and a pleasant lake view in front. Both sets of private apartments, hers and Guangxu's, contain contemporary Qing furniture.

The End of an Era

Two days after I entered the palace Tzu Hsi died, and on December 2, the "Great Ceremony of Enthronement" took place, a ceremony that I ruined with my crying.

The ceremony took place in the Hall of Supreme Harmony (Tai Ho Tien). Before it began I had to receive the obeisances of the commanders of the palace guard and ministers of the inner court in the Hall of Central Harmony (Chung Ho Tien) and the homage of the leading civilian and military officials. I found all this long and tiresome; it was moreover a very cold day, so when they carried me into the Hall of Supreme Harmony and put me up on the high and enormous throne I could bear it no longer. My father, who was kneeling below the throne and supporting me, told me not to fidget, but I struggled and cried, "I don't like it here. I want to go home. I don't like it here. I want to go home." My father grew so desperate that he was pouring with sweat. As the officials went on kotowing to me my cries grew louder and louder. My father tried to soothe me by saying, "Don't cry, don't cry; it'll soon be finished, it'll soon be finished."

When the ceremony was over the officials asked each other surreptitiously, "How could he say 'It'll soon be finished'? What does it mean, his saying he wanted to go home?" All these discussions took place in a very gloomy atmosphere as if these words had been a bad omen. Some books said that these words were prophetic as within three years the Ching Dynasty was in fact "finished" and the boy who wanted to "go home" did go home, and claimed that the officials had a presentiment of this.

Pu Yi, From Emperor to Citizen, *translated by W J F Jenner*

Another part of the compound is the Court of Virtuous Harmony (Deheyuan), made up of the Hall for Cultivating Happiness (Yiledian) and a theatre, built at the cost of 700,000 taels of silver to commemorate Cixi's 60th birthday. She was inordinately fond of theatricals and *tableaux vivants*, and even appeared in them herself. In this theatre a water tank had been sunk under the stage in order to provide such touches of verisimilitude as trickling streams and gushing fountains. The building, now renovated as a theatre museum, should not be missed. Attendants dressed in Qing-Dynasty clothes are on hand to direct visitors to superb exhibitions of theatre costumes and stage props. A collection of Cixi's personal possessions is also on display. These include the automobile—the first imported into China—presented by Yuan Shikai, the military commander who was later President of the new Republic for a brief time; silver and gold ware; brushes, garments and perfumes. The Hall for Cultivating Happiness now displays over 200 historical artefacts, among them the four large carved screens inlaid with jade which are considered national treasures.

Kunming Lake's Northern Shore
From the *pailou* (ceremonial arch) on the northern shore of Kunming Lake, the Cloud-Dispelling Hall (Paiyundian), the Hall of Virtuous Brilliance (Dehuidian), the Pavilion of Buddhist Incense (Foxiangge) and the Temple of the Sea of Wisdom (Zhihuihai) rise straight up the slope of Longevity Hill. Inside the Cloud-Dispelling Hall, where Cixi celebrated her birthdays, are displays of *penjing* (potted miniature landscapes) and artefacts which were almost all tributes from her ministers. The oil painting of the empress was executed by an American for Cixi's 69th birthday (see page 94).

The Long Corridor
Following the shoreline of the lake, the Long Corridor—730 metres (2,550 feet) in length—leads from the Hall of Happy Longevity to the ferry pier beside the Marble Boat. All along it views of the lake mingle with pictures of birds and flowers, scenes from legends and famous landscapes that have been painted on the beams of the roofed walk. The Chinese like to compare the promenade with a picture gallery, and say that so beguiling is the beauty that no courting couple can emerge at the other end unbetrothed.

South Lake Isle
From beside the Marble Boat (actually made of stone), below the Summer Palace's popular lunch restaurant Pavilion for Listening to the Orioles, it is possible to take a ferry across the water to the South Lake Isle (Nanhu Dao) and the Dragon King's Temple (Longwangmiao). From Nanhu you can walk across the Seventeen-Arch Bridge (Shiqikongqiao) back to the entrance.

The Summer Palace is open from 7 am to 7 pm (9 pm in summer). Entrance tickets are sold up to 5.30 pm.

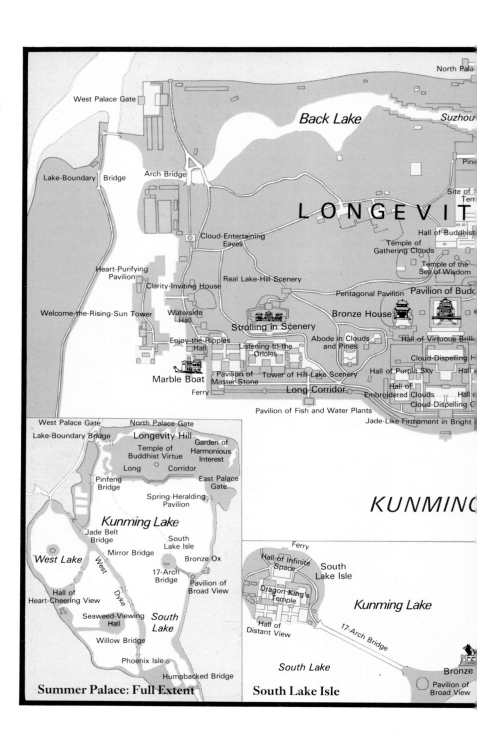

North Pala

West Palace Gate

Back Lake

Suzhou

Arch Bridge

Lake-Boundary Bridge

Pine

Site of
Ten

L O N G E V I T

Cloud-Entertaining
Eaves

Hall of Buddhist

Temple of
Gathering Clouds

Heart-Purifying
Pavilion

Temple of the
Sea of Wisdom

Clarity-Inviting House

Real Lake-Hill Scenery

Pentagonal Pavilion   Pavilion of Budd

Welcome-the-Rising-Sun Tower

Waterside
Hall

Bronze House

Enjoy-the-Ripples
Hall

Strolling in Scenery

Hall of Virtuous Brilli

Listening-to-the-
Orioles

Abode in Clouds
and Pines

Cloud-Dispelling H

Marble Boat

Pavilion of   Tower of Hill-Lake Scenery
Master Stone

Hall of Purple Sky   Hall

Ferry

Long Corridor

Hall of
Embroidered Clouds   Hall

Pavilion of Fish and Water Plants

Cloud-Dispelling G

Jade-Like Firmament in Bright

West Palace Gate   North Palace Gate

Lake-Boundary Bridge

Longevity Hill

Temple of
Buddhist Virtue

Garden of
Harmonious
Interest

Long   o   Corridor

Pinfeng
Bridge

East Palace
Gate

Spring-Heralding
Pavilion

Kunming Lake

KUNMING

Jade Belt
Bridge

South
Lake Isle

Mirror Bridge

West Lake

Bronze Ox

17-Arch
Bridge

Ferry

Hall of Infinite
Space

South
Lake Isle

Pavilion of
Broad View

Hall of
Heart-Cheering View

West

Dyke

Dragon King's
Temple

Kunming Lake

Seaweed-Viewing
Hall

South
Lake

17-Arch Bridge

Willow Bridge

Hall of
Distant View

Phoenix Isle

South Lake

Bronze

Humpbacked Bridge

Pavilion of
Broad View

Summer Palace: Full Extent

South Lake Isle

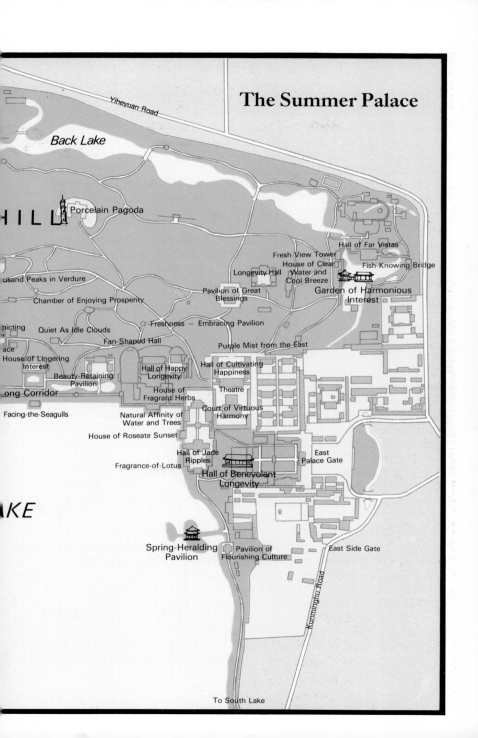

The Summer Palace

Yiheyuan Road

Back Lake

HILL

Porcelain Pagoda

Hall of Far Vistas

Fresh View Tower
House of Clear
Longevity Hall   Water and
Cool Breeze   Fish-Knowing Bridge

usand Peaks in Verdure

Pavilion of Great
Blessings

Garden of Harmonious
Interest

Chamber of Enjoying Prosperity

picting
g   Quiet As Idle Clouds
ace
House of Lingering
Interest

Freshness — Embracing Pavilion

Fan-Shaped Hall

Purple Mist from the East

Beauty-Retaining
Pavilion

Hall of Happy
Longevity

Hall of Cultivating
Happiness

ong Corridor

House of
Fragrant Herbs

Theatre

Facing-the-Seagulls

Natural Affinity of
Water and Trees

Court of Virtuous
Harmony

House of Roseate Sunset

Hall of Jade
Ripples

East
Palace Gate

Fragrance-of-Lotus

Hall of Benevolent
Longevity

KE

Spring-Heralding
Pavilion

Pavilion of
Flourishing Culture

East Side Gate

Kunminghu Road

To South Lake

The Old Summer Palace (Yuanmingyuan)

Not far from the Yiheyuan is the site of the old Qing Summer Palace, Yuanmingyuan. Little is left of it now except some broken pillars and masonry lying about in a field. There is a museum—the Garden History Exhibition Hall—with a well-arranged display of drawings and models showing the splendour of the palace in its heyday.

The museum is part of a recent effort to turn the site into a public park, with some shrubs, trees and a few paths for the many citizens of Beijing—who can bicycle here in about half an hour—seeking respite from their urban surroundings.

In the late 1980s, a French consortium of historians and architects reconstructed the maze in concrete. For years there have been plans afoot to rebuild the entire palace as a sort of Qing-dynasty Disneyland. But a conservative faction opposed this idea on the grounds that it was a better lesson for China and the world if this monument of Chinese splendour and foreign imperialist destruction remained in fragments rather than turn the place into a commercial spectacle.

The Temple of the Sleeping Buddha (Wofosi)

This temple, 19 kilometres (12 miles) from the city, is reached by continuing west on the road from the Summer Palace towards the Fragrant Hills, passing Jade Spring Hill with its distinctive twin pagodas.

There is mention in the historical records of an enormous statue of the recumbent Buddha first being cast at the temple in the 14th century, but the present statue probably dates from a later period. The Buddha, in lacquered bronze, lying full length with his head supported by his right arm, is five metres (16 feet) long. Enormous shoes which have been presented to the Buddha are displayed in cases on either side. Some rare trees grow in the surrounding countryside, and a line of ancient evergreens leads up to the temple's portico.

The Temple of Azure Clouds (Biyunsi)

A short way from the Temple of the Sleeping Buddha on the road leading to the Fragrant Hills is one of Beijing's great temples, the Temple of Azure Clouds. A temple has stood here since the Yuan Dynasty. It was restored and extended on two separate occasions by palace eunuchs Yu Jing and Wei Zhongxian, who planned to place their graves in the hill behind (they both failed in their ambition). There are many buildings here, arranged on the side of a hill, and much to see. At the top of the hill is the Diamond Throne Pagoda, an Indian-style stone temple with a spectacular view from its roof. It was built on the lines of the Five Pagoda Temple (see page 111) in 1792. Below is the Memorial Hall to Sun Yat-sen. After his death in 1925 the body of the founder of modern China lay in state in this temple, reposing in a crystal coffin presented by the Soviet Union. His body was moved to Nanjing in 1929 when the mausoleum there had been completed.

To one side of the Memorial Hall is the Luohan Hall, with its four inner courtyards, which was built in the mid-18th century. *Luohan* are the disciples of Buddha, and over 500 gilded wooden statues of these proselytes, each one quite distinct with an individual, and very human, personality, are crammed into this section of the temple complex.

Biyunsi, open between 8 am and 5 pm, makes for a particularly delightful excursion in the spring, when the peach and almond trees—both within the temple complex and on the surrounding hillsides—are covered in blossom.

Fragrant Hills Park (Xiangshan Gongyuan)

Close to the Temple of Azure Clouds, this park is set in a belt of hills northwest of Beijing, about 40 minutes' drive away. The Western Hills, as the area is also called, has long been a favourite retreat of the emperors. In the 12th century when it was a royal hunting park, the landscape was considered so picturesque that the hills came to be designated as one of the Eight Great Scenes of Yanjing (the City of Swallows). With the addition of a resort palace in the reign of Kangxi, its attractions further increased until the park reached the peak of its splendour in the 18th century.

Roads fan out from the main east-facing gate. To the left is the Fragrant Hills Hotel, a recent construction. Many of the old beauty spots still remain, however, most notably at the northern end of the park. One can reach this part by entering through the north gate from the direction of the Temple of Azure Clouds. Crossing Glass Lake (Yanjinghu) one comes to the Study of Self-knowledge (Jianxinzhai), a 16th-century garden with a circular pool, enclosed by a rounded wall and promenade and shielded by clumps of trees on three sides. To the south of it are the remains of Zhaomiao, a Tibetan-style temple erected in the Qianlong period, as well as an ornamental archway and a pagoda roofed in yellow glazed tiles,with bells dangling from its eaves. There is now a cable car which takes visitors to the top in 18 minutes and which costs Rmb3 each way.

The name 'Fragrant Hills' probably derives from the two slabs of stone—shaped like incense burners—on top of the highest peak at the western extremity of the park. The wisps of mist clinging to the summit resemble, it is claimed, puffs of scented smoke coming from the incense burners at the top. But the park is famous above all for its autumn aspect. The blaze of red on the hillsides when the leaves of the Huanglu smoke tree (sometimes referred to as maple) are turning is a sight that has been celebrated in poetry and painting.

The North
The Great Wall (Changcheng)

The Great Wall, said to be the only man-made structure visible from the moon, has captured the imagination of countless people throughout its long history.

The wall was built in a piecemeal fashion over a long period, from the fifth century BC down to the 16th century AD, as a means of defence against raids from northern nomadic tribes. When the empire was unified under Qin Shi Huangdi in 221 BC, a continuous line of fortifications was ordered to be constructed by joining up the old walls.

'A wall between is a mountain' goes an old saying, and in the hearts of the Chinese, the 'Wall of Ten-thousand Li' (Wanli Changcheng) not only protected them from the barbaric Huns (Xiongnu), its significance lay also in separating the familiar, safe, patterns of settled agriculture, from the alien pastoral nomadic life of the steppes and deserts beyond.

Historical texts record as many as 300,000 men working for ten years on the construction of a section of the wall. Stories of the hardship suffered by these conscripted labourers have been passed down, contributing to the image of the Qin emperor as a hated tyrant. Built partly of earth faced with brick and partly of masonry, the Great Wall stretched for 4,000 kilometres (2,500 miles) from Central Asia to the Yellow Sea. It was lined with ramparts and punctuated by watchtowers, from which smoke signals were sent to the capital at Xi'an by sentries posted at the wall's strategic points.

The Great Wall has fallen into disrepair and then been rebuilt many times through the centuries. In recent years three parts of the wall have been restored. Visitors to Beijing usually go to the section at **Badaling**, in Nankou Pass, about 80 kilometres (50 miles) from the city, either before or after a visit to the Ming Tombs. There is a special train service from Beijing to Badaling, which runs daily in the summer and several times a week off-season. The train goes from Xizhimen station in northwest Beijing (not the main railway station) and tickets can be bought on board. It is also possible to travel up to the wall by taxi or coach, as long as the road is not blocked by snow. CITS and the major hotels organize their own tours. The drive takes around two hours.

The road to the Great Wall passes through the Juyongguan, or Juyong Pass, where there is a stunning white marble structure known as the Cloud Platform. Built in 1345 during the Yuan dynasty, it originally served as the base for three pagodas which were destroyed several decades later. The platform is pierced by a hexagonal archway. The ceiling and walls are covered with wonderful carvings of the Four Heavenly Kings and the texts of Buddhist scriptures in six languages: Nepalese Sanskrit, Tibetan, Phags-pa Mongolian, Uighur, Xi Xia and Han Chinese.

It is extremely cold on the wall in winter, but it is also at its most impressive at this time, when the mountains are covered with snow. In any season, the ideal time to go would be after 3 pm (when all the crowds have left) by arranging one's own transport (Rmb220–250 by taxi).

The restored section of Badaling dates from the Ming. From the carpark it is possible to climb up onto the wall, and walk either to the left or right.

The newest section of the Great Wall to have been restored is at **Mutianyu**, northwest of Beijing in Huairou county. The major advantage to visiting this section of the wall is that it is far less crowded than that at Badaling because most people must get there by chartered bus or car. There is a long distance bus available at Dongzhimen Long Distance Bus Station each morning at 7 am, returning mid-afternoon.

Before reaching the wall one has to mount some thousand steps or ride the funicular. This expanse of the wall trails off for more than a mile and unlike Badaling, one has an unobstructed view in both directions of great lengths of the wall undulating along mountain crests until they fade into the distance. Here there is a much more peaceful atmosphere and one can really get a sense of the Great Wall's history and grandeur as it spans the horizon.

A third site for climbing on the Great Wall is located at **Simatai**, approximately 15 kilometres (ten miles) northwest of Miyun Reservoir. On clear nights, it is possible to see the lights of Beijing from here.

Two new tourist destinations have been opened up in the vicinity of Badaling. **Longqing Gorge**, in Yanqing county north of the Yanqing county seat, is the site of a winter ice lantern exhibition held in January and February.

The Garden of Perfection and Brightness

The ruins of the old Qing Summer Palace, Yuanmingyuan, barely conjure up the former glory of the 'Garden of Gardens'. Yuanmingyuan—the garden of Perfection and Brightness—was first established by Emperor Yongzheng (reigned 1723–35), although several gardens had existed on this site since the Ming Dynasty.

From the Ming to the early Qing, garden-making gained enormous popularity and the art of taming disordered landscape and yet preserving its 'naturalness' reached the height of sophistication in the reign of Emperor Qianlong.

The northwestern suburbs of Beijing, stretching right up to the Fragrant Hills, must have appeared eminently suitable for exercising this art. The area is a large plain where terrain and natural springs provided ideal conditions for creating the private gardens and lavish resorts that came to be established there. The Fragrant Hills resort palace was one of these; the Garden of Carefree Spring (Changchunyuan) was another. In due course the whole area became almost totally the exclusive pleasure grounds of emperors and their kinsmen.

Changchunyuan was more than an imperial garden. Emperor Kangxi had a palace built so that he could administer State affairs there as well as in the Forbidden City. To the north of Changchunyuan was Yuanmingyuan, a private garden bestowed on Prince Yinzhen, Kangxi's fourth son, in 1709. On Yinzhen's accession, he embarked on a massive project to extend and transform Yuanmingyuan into a resort fit for an emperor. The Auspicious Sea (Fuhai) was excavated at that time. Water was in fact the dominant theme of the garden and extensively used by landscape artists in designing architectural groupings, scenic spots or formal views. From the time Prince Yinzhen ascended the throne as the Yongzhen Emperor, five successive rulers moved their Court to Yuanmingyuan after each New Year. Except for excursions to Chengde during the summer, they lived in Yuanmingyuan until the winter solstice.

Under Emperor Qianlong, Yuanmingyuan became even more splendid. From his inspection tours of the area around the Yangzi River, the emperor assimilated and then transplanted garden-making ideas and scenery from the south. Although 69 'scenes' or 'views' were created in the Summer Palace, 40 of them were recorded by Yongzhen's Court painters Shen Yuan and Tang Dai, and it is from these scrolls that historians have reconstructed a broader picture of this outstanding garden. Descriptions of it have also survived in the correspondence of the Catholic missionaries employed by the Qing Court. One of them, the Jesuit artist Giuseppe Castiglione, was commissioned by Qianlong in 1745 to design the European-style Western Mansions (Xiyanglou) that were constructed along the northern wall. It is the ruins of these extraordinary palaces that remain today.

In 1860 when Anglo-French troops captured Beijing, rampaging soldiers, on the orders of Lord Elgin, set fire to Yuanmingyuan. A young captain of the British Royal Engineers, who was later to gain fame as 'Chinese Gordon', wrote after the destruction: '[We] went out, and, after pillaging it, burned the whole place, destroying in a Vandal-like manner most valuable property which would not be replaced for four millions. We got upwards of £48 a-piece prize money before we went out here; and although I have not as much as many, I have done well.

'The people are civil, but I think the grandees hate us, as they must after what we did to the Palace. You can scarcely imagine the beauty and magnificence of the places we burnt. It made one's heart sore to burn them; in fact, these palaces were so large, and we were so pressed for time, that we could not plunder them carefully. Quantities of gold ornaments were burnt, considered as brass. It was wretchedly demoralizing work for an army. Everybody was wild for plunder.'

Thirteen years later an attempt was made to rebuild the palace to mark Empress Dowager Cixi's 40th birthday, but dwindling funds put a full-scale restoration out of the question. It was once again devastated in 1900, this time by the Allied Expeditionary Force who relieved the Siege of the Legations. Over the years the damage was compounded by local peasants scavenging for building materials.

In 1977 maintenance of the ruins of Yuanmingyuan was put in the charge of the Beijing municipal authorities, and a small museum has been set up at the site to show the scale and magnificence of the palace in its day. Despite these efforts at conservation, the area remains a wilderness with a few romantic rococo ruins for children to climb on when families picnic there. Energetic Beijing residents say that the best time to visit Yuanmingyuan is at dawn. To many other Chinese it remains a powerful symbol of imperial folly and western aggression.

The **Kangxi Grassland** (no relation to the Qing-dynasty emperor of the same name) on the shores of Guanting Reservoir, features swimming, fishing and horseback riding on ex-army horses and Mongolian ponies.

A further Great Wall site has been opened to tourists at Huangyaguan, approximately three hours away from Beijing, near the Eastern Qing Tombs in Hebei Province.

The Ming Tombs (Ming Shisanling)

The valley of the Ming Tombs lies about 48 kilometres (30 miles) north of Beijing. Thirteen of the 16 Ming emperors are interred here, hence the site's Chinese name, Ming Shisanling (The 13 Ming Tombs). The tombs were located in accordance with Chinese geomantic specifications requiring graves to be protected by high ground.

The approach is impressive. The modern road passes by a stone portico with five carved archways. This is the beginning of the imposing route known as the Spirit (or Sacred) Way. Next comes the Great Vermilion Gateway; of its three openings the central entrance was reserved for the coffins of deceased emperors, and all followers were required to dismount at this point. The whole tomb site, to which this gateway was the actual entrance, was of course surrounded by a wall, now gone.

The Spirit Way

The emperor's coffin would have been borne past a stele pavilion, a typical imperial structure with the floating clouds motif repeated on its supporting columns. The procession of mourners would then have filed along the Spirit Way, a funeral guard of honour of six pairs of animals and six pairs of human figures carved from large blocks of stone. The latter, all standing, are statues of scholars, administrators and warriors. The animals—lions, *xiechi* (a mythical beast), camels, elephants, unicorns, horses—are either standing or crouching. The Spirit Way ends at the Dragon and Phoenix Gate.

In its entirety, this part of the Ming Tombs dates from the 15th century. Beside the road there is now a mass of shrubs and fruit trees. Once across an arched bridge, visitors can then visit the different tombs, scattered round the valley.

Changling

The most important tomb, appropriately, belongs to the great Yongle, the third Ming emperor, who was responsible for building so much of Beijing. He chose this site and had his burial place built on the traditional plan of a walled enclave, enclosing buildings separated by three courtyards, with the tumulus at its head.

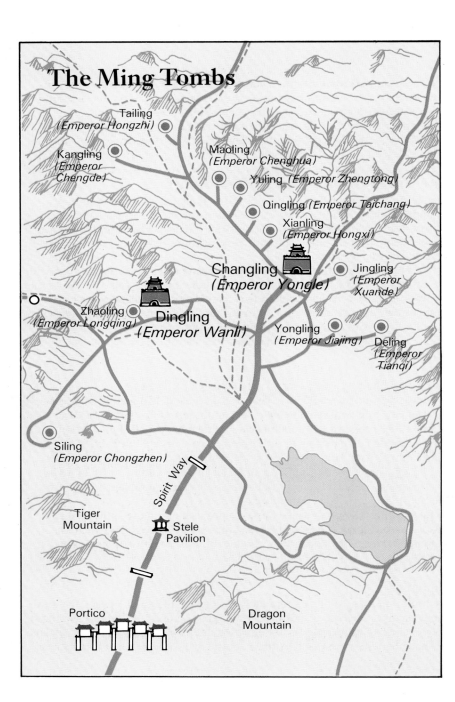

The Ming Tombs

Tailing
(Emperor Hongzhi)

Kangling
*(Emperor
Chengde)*

Maoling
(Emperor Chenghua)

Yuling *(Emperor Zhengtong)*

Qingling *(Emperor Taichang)*

Xianling
(Emperor Hongxi)

Changling
(Emperor Yongle)

Jingling
*(Emperor
Xuande)*

Zhaoling
(Emperor Longqing)   Dingling
(Emperor Wanli)

Yongling
(Emperor Jiajing)

Deling
*(Emperor
Tianqi)*

Siling
(Emperor Chongzhen)

Spirit Way

Tiger
Mountain

Stele
Pavilion

Portico

Dragon
Mountain

The tumulus, marked by a stele tower and traditionally referred to as the Precious Fortress (Baocheng), has not been excavated, but visitors may see inside the magnificent Hall of Sacrifice. This very fine structure built in 1427 is supported by 32 massive wooden pillars wrought from huge trunks of *nanmu* wood from the extreme southwest of China. The Yongle Emperor was interred in the Changling in 1424. Sixteen royal concubines were buried alive in ancillary graves following a custom that was finally discontinued during the reign of the sixth Ming emperor.

Dingling

The tomb of the Wanli Emperor (reigned 1573–1620) and his two consorts is known as the Dingling. Its construction was started in 1584, when Wanli was 22, and took six years to complete. It was excavated in 1958, and one may now descend by a modern spiral staircase to the underground tomb behind a stele tower.

The vaulted marble palace, built deep underground so that it is cool in summer and comfortably warm in winter, consists of three burial chambers. At

Pailous

To get to the Temple of Confucius and the Former Imperial College, you will pass under at least one of the few extant street *pailous* in Beijing. Before modern transport made it necessary to reduce their numbers greatly, *pailous* decorated many streets and intersections in Beijing and other cities in northern China. In Beijing, for example, Xidan means 'western single' and refers to a single *pailou* that once stood at the intersection of West Chan'anjie and Xidan beidajie, while Xisi, literally 'western four' reminds us that there were once four *pailous* at the intersection that is still referred to by that name.

Some scholars trace the origin of the *pailou* to India, where *toranas*, two columns (posts) with several decorative crossbeams (lintols), were placed at the gateways of temples. There is a striking resemblance between the stone gateways surrounding the large hemispherical stupa at Sanchi, and those at the Round Altar in the Temple of Heaven in Beijing. Later *pailous* have highly elaborate (and often ungainly) wooden superstructures with manifold roofs, always in odd numbers, and sometimes covered with glazed tiles.

In residential districts, *pailous* were erected to commemorate virtuous women or heroic men. No such *pailous* have survived in Beijing.

Pailous can be seen in the Temple of Confucius, Imperial College, Lama temple, Beihai Park and the Summer Palace, to mention a few. The marble *pailou* at the entrance to the Ming Tombs, once painted a brilliant red and green, is regarded as one of the finest in China.

the entrance to the antechamber is a carved marble gateway. The floor is paved with specially made 'golden bricks' which had been fired for 130 days and dipped in tung oil before being laid. The middle chamber contains three marble thrones; in front of each of them are five drumshaped stools for holding offerings and a large glazed pot known as the Ever Bright Lamp. The lamps would have been filled with oil and lit before the tomb was sealed. The back chamber was the actual repository of the royal coffins.

On being opened by the excavation team they were found to be stuffed with some 300 assorted garments. Even more lavish, countless pieces of jewellery, curios and porcelain—stowed in 26 lacquer chests—were also deposited to provide for a luxurious life in the nether world. The regalia and the treasure have all been moved to two small exhibition halls outside. They should not be missed.

Another modern addition to the valley of the Ming Tombs has recently been opened— it is a golf course laid out by Japanese investors.

Shen Zhou Doggy Park

You have to see it to believe it, but this canine zoo might be just what you need if you are fed up with Qianlong and the Empress Dowager—although this is precisely the sort of place the obsessive Old Buddha might build for herself.

Located in the town of Shahe (in Caihe xincun; tel. 9733342) about 30 kilometres (19 miles) north of the city on the road to Changping county, the Shen Zhou Doggy Park brings together some 60 breeds of dog in palatial surroundings. The native barkers are all here: sharpeis, Pekingese, Lhasa dogs, chowchows and Tibetan mastiffs, as well as British boxers, Mexican chihuahuas and French poodles. One of the items on the programme is revealing: military and police dogs 'catching enemies' and 'helping their owners in danger'. The Doggy Park supplies the Public Security Bureau. It opened in 1990 and has all the makings of a Beijing institution. Bring the kiddies.

Other notable services include dog cart rides and a dog clinic, presided over by a Dog King and Dog Queen with their civil and military attendants. Although dog is eaten as a winter delicacy in some parts of China, there is no public dog restaurant here.

The East

The Eastern Qing Tombs (Dongling)

The site of the Eastern Qing Tombs is over the provincial border, in Hebei, some 121 kilometres (75 miles) east of Beijing (a journey of about four hours by car).

The 15 tombs are spread over an area 34 kilometres (21 miles) wide, and built under the lee of Mount Changrui. The choice of this site as the Qing imperial burial ground is attributed to the Shunzhi emperor, who came upon it when out hunting. He is interred here, together with the Kangxi, Qianlong, Xianfeng and Tongzhi emperors. Other tombs include those of the Empress Dowager Cixi, several less notorious empresses, concubines and royal children, as well as that of Emperor Kangxi's revered teacher.

There are some striking differences between the Ming and Qing tombs. Whereas the Ming created a single 'Spirit Way' (the approach to imperial burial grounds lined with stone animals and officials), the Qing have several shorter ones leading to tumuli which are also on a smaller scale. The Qing stone figures have their hair in the traditional Manchu plait, and while the scholar is shown wearing a string of beads of Buddhist origin, emblematic of the strong lamaistic leanings of the Manchu rulers, the Ming statues are generally depicted carrying Confucian tablets. The animals too differ in style and decoration.

The tombs of the Qianlong Emperor, the Empress Ci'an and the Empress Dowager Cixi are open to the public. The underground marble vault of Qianlong is particularly impressive: every interior wall and arch is richly carved with images of the Buddha, the Celestial Guardians and with thousands of words of Buddhist scriptures in both Sanskrit and Tibetan. Ornate carving also embellishes Cixi's mausoleum, where one can see the repeated use of such imperial motifs as dragons, phoenixes and clouds. Built over a period of 30 years, the tomb was a subject of great interest to the Empress Dowager, who visited the site several times. Unfortunately both this tomb and that of the Qianlong emperor were broken into by grave robbers in the 1920s, and the fabulous treasures, buried with the view of ensuring a comfortable afterlife, have all disappeared.

Visitors may like to round off their excursion to the Dongling by calling in at the two small museums that have been established in the sacrificial halls at the tombs of the two empresses, Cixi and Ci'an. Opening times are from 9 am to 4 pm.

The Southwest

Marco Polo Bridge (Lugouqiao)

Proceeding southwest from Guang'anmenwai for about 16 kilometres (ten miles), one reaches the Lugouqiao, celebrated not only for being Beijing's oldest surviving bridge, but also for the impression it made on Marco Polo, who saw it in 1290 (hence the bridge's western name). He has left us with a fine description.

Marco Polo Bridge spans the Yongding River. As early as the Warring States period (475–221 BC), the site of the present bridge had been a strategically important river crossing. Initially the crossing was probably made by a wooden bridge or by pontoons. From the Jin Dynasty onwards, when the capital was at Beijing, increased traffic across the river warranted a more permanent bridge, which was completed in 1192. Constructed with careful reference to the river's flow, this solid stone structure resting on 11 arches has withstood weathering for several centuries. The piers supporting the bridge are specially strong, being reinforced by triangular metal posts which locals used to call 'Swords for Decapitating Dragons' in the belief that evil dragons, seeing these posts, would quietly go away rather than cause mischief for river craft.

On either side of the bridge there is a parapet with 140 columns carved and surmounted with lions. Imperial steles stand at each end; one commemorates the renovation of the bridge in 1698, the other carries a four-character inscription by Emperor Qianlong, 'Bright Moon on Lugou'.

Peking Man Site

The village of Zhoukoudian, which can be reached by train from Beijing, used to be notable for its production of lime. In 1929 it achieved worldwide fame with the discovery of the first skulls of Peking Man. The fossil remains of *Homo erectus pekinensis* have been dated to about 300,000–500,000 years ago.

The limestone caves of Zhoukoudian probably account for the location of a paleolithic settlement here. So far bones of over 40 inhabitants have been unearthed and, with the evidence of other remains, scientists have pieced together a fascinating picture of this early community.

Some of the limestone caves, on the northern slope of Dragon Bones Hills (Longgushan) to the east of Zhoukoudian station, may be visited. There is also a comprehensive museum on the evolution of man and the Zhoukoudian culture. Included in the displays are stone implements used by Peking Man and Upper Cave Man (who lived about 50,000 years ago), fossils of animals hunted by them, and evidence that Peking Man used fire. The whereabouts of the original Peking Man fossils, lost during the Second World War while en route to the United States for safekeeping, is still however shrouded in mystery.

Zhoukoudian is 48 kilometres (30 miles) to the southwest of Beijing. It is best to go with a tour guide as very little information is available in English at the site.

Daboatai Han Tomb

Located about 15 kilometres (ten miles) from the city limits in the Fengtai district, the Dabaotai Han-dynasty tomb is a worthwhile half-day outing. Difficult to locate on account of a lack of road signs, the best way to get there is to take a taxi (there is no public transport) to the village of Guogongzhuang and ask the way from there. Dabaotai is about four kilometres (two-and-a-half miles) directly south of the Fengtai Railway Station.

The archaeologists who excavated the tomb in 1975 are unable to determine who was buried in this spectacular underground 'wooden palace', but the choice has been narrowed down to one of two princes belonging to the Liu clan who died approximately 50 BC.

The excellently restored tomb consists of three inner and outer coffins of wood, surrounded by a boundary wall built up of tens of thousands of square wooden beams. The wall of the tomb was further lined with a boundary wall of heaped beams, and sealed with a thick layer of plaster to keep it dry, which partially explains its excellent state of preservation. The entire tomb is 23.2 metres (80 feet) long, 18 metres (56 feet) wide and 4.7 metres (14.5 feet) deep and has been enclosed in a poorly lit building. The most extraordinary objects on view are the three lacquered chariots and 11 horses that were buried alive with them in a long narrow chamber that stands at the entrance to the tomb. A second tomb containing the remains of the queen consort was plundered and burnt in ancient times and nothing is left of it except the site.

Newly built models of the chariots are on display in a separate hall, and there is a small museum containing some of the burial objects found in the tomb, including jade carvings, miniature wooden burial figures, bronze incense burners and a bronze door decoration in the form of a grotesque beast.

The West

Western Qing Tombs (Xiling)

Like the Eastern Qing Tombs (see page 133), the Western Qing Tombs lie a good distance from the capital, some 125 kilometres (78 miles) southwest of the city in Yixian, Hebei Province. Four emperors—Yongzheng, Jiaqing, Daoguang and Guangxu—are buried here, along with three empresses, seven princes and a handful of imperial concubines.

One traditional view holds that Yongzheng (reigned 1723–35), son of the great Kangxi and father of the great Qianlong, chose to be buried apart from his father because he had ascended the throne by devious means, but there is little evidence to support this. In any case, Qianlong decreed that after his own death the tombs of the emperors that came after him should be distributed alternatively between the eastern and western burial grounds. Incidentally, Puyi, the last emperor of the Qing dynasty, is the only Qing Son of Heaven not to be buried there at all; he was cremated after his death in 1967, and his ashes placed in the revolutionary cemetery at Babaoshan.

The Tailing, the tomb of Yongzheng, is the largest tomb in the entire mausoleum complex. It consists of numerous gateways and buildings that were used during the various Buddhist rituals and sacrifices held in the emperor's memory.

The Muling of the Emperor Daoguang (reigned 1821–50) is small in comparison to the Tailing but is more exquisitely constructed. Soon after his ascension to the throne, Daoguang began building his tomb at the eastern burial grounds, as decreed by Qianlong. One year after its completion, however, the underground burial chamber was found to be flooded, and Daoguang, finding this inauspicious, went in person to the Western Tombs to select a new site for himself.

Because Daoguang believed that the flooding in his first tomb had occurred because several dragons had been deprived of their homes, he was very lavish in decorating his second tomb with carved images of this auspicious creature.

The Chongling of Emperor Guangxu (reigned 1875–1908) was left unfinished when the Qing dynasty fell in 1911, and it was only completed four years later. Accompanying Guangxu in a tomb of her own are the remains of Zhenfei, known in English as the Pearl Concubine, Guangxu's favourite. Zhenfei was forced down a well in the Imperial Palace and died by the order of the jealous Empress Dowager Cixi before she fled Beijing in the aftermath of the Boxer Uprising.

138

Gateway within the Forbidden City (below);
Dragon and Cloud balustrade (above right);
River of Golden Water(below right)

The Temple of the Pool and Wild Mulberry (Tanzhesi)

Situated in the Western Hills, this Buddhist temple lies 45 kilometres (28 miles) west of Beijing. It is reached by a winding road which passes the Ordination Terrace Temple (see page 139) and some quite spectacular scenery, especially in the spring when the fruit trees are in blossom. One of the biggest and oldest temples in the Beijing area, Tanzhesi has been completely restored in recent years.

A temple known by various names has existed on this site for 1,600 years. Its present name is derived from the Dragon Pool nearby and from the trees, growing on the hillside, whose leaves were used to feed silkworms. The present structure, laid out on traditional lines, is typical of Ming and Qing architecture. A ceremonial arch (*pailou*) frames the entrance to a compound of several halls, pavilions and courtyards: there is the Hall of Abstinence, the Ordination Altar and, at the back of it, the Hall to Guanyin, the Goddess of Mercy. The latter is associated with Kublai Khan's daughter, Princess Miaoyan, who entered the

nunnery here in the 13th century. Her devotions were performed so assiduously, it is said, that she wore deep marks into the piece of stone on which she stood.

Some of the strangely shaped trees within the temple are said to be a thousand years old.

To the right of the Hall of Abstinence is the Flowing Cup Pavilion (Liubeiting), where dragon-shaped channels feed spring water into the Dragon Pool. This water has a special quality which enables objects to float upon the surface easily. On the third day of the third month people used to gather for the 'purification of the fermented wine'; brimming wine cups were floated down the stream and only when they stopped moving was the wine drunk.

Below the temple are beautiful stone stupas built over the burial sites of the temple's monks dating from the Jin, Yuan, Ming and Qing Dynasties.

The Ordination Terrace Temple (Jietaisi)

The temple lies in the Western Hills, 33 kilometres (22 miles) from Beijing on the road that leads to the Temple of the Pool and Wild Mulberry. There has been a temple in this mountain cleft for 1,350 years, but it was in the Liao Dynasty (916–1125) that its chief function—the ordination of Buddhist novices—was established when a monk, Fajun, founded an altar here.

The Ordination Altar, in the northeast courtyard, is of white marble and its three tiers are carved with hundreds of figures, some as tall as a metre (just over three feet). Once a year, at midnight, an initiation ceremony was conducted; the novices, having fasted all day, would endure burns from lighted incense sticks upon their tonsured heads.

As the temple was one of his favoured rest-stops, the Qing emperor Qianlong handsomely endowed it during his reign, and the present buildings contribute to the temple's peculiar charm. One of them, which sadly no longer survives, is marked with a stone tablet which can be seen to the left of the Thousand Buddha Pavilion behind the temple's main hall. In the time of Qianlong this remakable pine was dubbed the 'Mobile Tree' on account of its ability to shake all over when any one of its branches was pulled.

Temple of the Sea of the Law (Fahaisi)

Located approximately two kilometres (one-and-a-half miles) northeast of Moshikou in the Shijingshan district, the Temple of the Sea of the Law can be visited at the same time as its neighbours, the Tanzhesi and Jietaisi.

According to an inscription in the temple, it was built in about 1440 by an eunuch in the court of the Ming Zhengtong emperor with funds he collected from various officials, lamas, monks, nuns and lay Buddhists. Its design is similar to that of other mountain temples, being laid out on three levels.

The finest works of art in the temple are the famous frescos painted on the interior walls of the Daxiongbaodian, which stands on the north side of the rear-most courtyard. The paintings are as old as the temple itself, and were executed by some 15 palace painters who are named on a stone tablet found near the temple.

The frescos show groups of emperors, empresses, and religious figures engaged in Buddhist worship, as well as the objects of their worship, the bodhisattvas Guanyin (Avalokitesvara), Wenshu (Manjushri) and Samantahbadra (Puxian). Note also the painted mandalas in the three cupolas in the ceiling of this hall. The lively, colourful and wonderfully detailed brush work are important monuments in the history of Chinese painting.

Museums
Palace Museum

Although the Imperial Palace in its entirety is regarded as a museum of architectural and artistic heritage, there are specific halls and pavilions within it—collectively known as the Palace Museum—which are used as showcases for the cornucopia of treasures in the palace. As the restoration of the Palace is constantly in progress, new areas of exhibits are opened from time to time.

Visiting hours are 8.30 am–4.30 pm with the ticket offices closing at 3.30 pm. However, the Museum of Imperial Treasures closes at 4.15 pm with the ticket office closing at 3.15 pm.

The Historical Art Museum

Housed in the Hall of Preserving Harmony (Baohedian), the collection here provides a broad conspectus of Chinese cultural development. Arranged chronologically, the exhibition is in three parts. The first part deals with the period from earliest times to about 4,000 years ago, illustrated by excavated ancient painted pottery, bronzes and sculptures. The fifth to the 13th centuries—the period covered by the second section—saw the emergence of an early modern style of painting as well as major developments in the art of ivory carving, lacquerware, weaving and calligraphy. The third part of the exhibition shows samples of the arts during the Yuan, Ming and Qing Dynasties; of particular interest is the fine porcelain that was produced in this era.

Several special exhibitions of imperial treasures are housed in the Six Eastern Palaces at the rear of the complex.

The Hall of Bronzes

This collection is shown in the Palace of Abstinence (Zhaigong), the Hall of Sincere Solemnity (Chengsudian) and the Palace of Revered Benevolence (Jingrengong), and includes examples of bronze wine goblets, tripod cooking vessels and pots from the Shang, Zhou, Spring and Autumn and Warring States periods

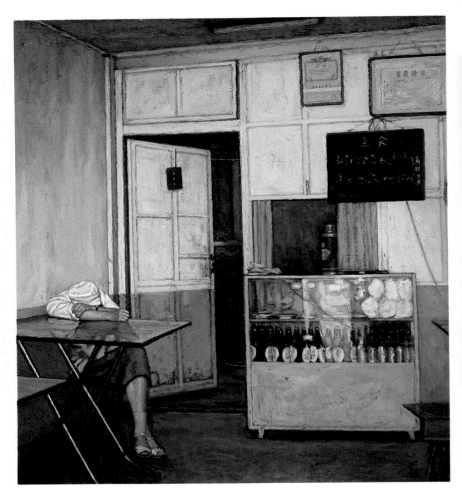

The Hall of Ceramics

The Palace of Heavenly Favours (Chengqiangong) and the Palace of Eternal Harmony (Yonghegong) contains Neolithic pottery from the Shang to the Western Zhou Dynasties, with examples of Longshan blackware, incised and glazed pottery from the Han Dynasty on through to the celadon ware of the Yuan, the tri-coloured glazes of the Tang and the blue and white of the Ming and Qing Dynasties. Many fine examples from the famous imperial kilns of Jingdezhen can be seen.

The Hall of Paintings

Scroll paintings and calligraphy are displayed in the Hall of Imperial Supremacy (Huangjidian), the Palace of Peaceful Old Age (Ningshougong) and galleries on its eastern, western and southern sides. For a few weeks each autumn, during the dry weather, the rarest examples of Chinese visual arts are brought out for public view.

The Museum of Imperial Treasures

This superb hoard of ritual and everyday items used by the Qing Court is displayed in the Hall of Character Cultivation (Yangxindian) and the Palace of Happy Old Age (Leshougong). The treasures grouped together in the first hall include silver and gold tableware, jewelled knick-knacks and little Buddhist shrines. The latter, generally made of gold, include one made for Emperor Qianlong to preserve a strand of his mother's hair.

In the second hall, which contains the gorgeous habiliments and attire worn
by emperors, empresses and concubines, there are exquisite pieces of jewellery,
hairpins and head-dresses as well as Court costumes. One of the most outstanding exhibits is Qianlong's peacock feather-trimmed robe studded with seed
pearls and tiny coral beads.

The sybaritic Court amassed a vast number of ornaments and decorative
pieces to adorn the palace interior. One kind of curio (which is still popular with
collectors today) is the jewelled *penjing*—artificial miniature potted landscapes
composed of precious stones, with leaves and petals carved out of gold, silver
and jade—which are shown in the third section.

Note that although the Museum of Imperial Treasures is open 8.30 am–4.30
pm daily, the ticket office closes at 3.15 pm.

The Hall of Clocks and Watches
A small gallery northeast of the Palace of Earthly Peace (Kunninggong) houses
an extraordinary collection of elaborate clocks, both European and Chinese,
dating from the 18th and 19th centuries.

Exhibition of Historical Relics from the Qing
Several aspects of imperial life and duties are represented by the relics here in
the Palace of Heavenly Purity (Qianqinggong), for example the imperial seals
for giving the stamp of royal approval to decrees issued in the emperor's name.
There are also musical instruments, more ceremonial and travelling regalia and
weapons and arms.

Museum of the Chinese Revolution and Museum of Chinese History
The large building which houses these two museums stands opposite the Great
Hall of the People, on the eastern side of Tiananmen Square. It is open 8.30 am–
5 pm (admission till 3 pm only) and is closed on Mondays.

Museum of the Chinese Revolution
This occupies the north (left) wing of the building. More than 3,300 exhibits,
displayed on two floors, illustrate the history of the Chinese Communist Party.
The collection of models, documents and materials begins with the May Fourth
Movement of 1919 and moves on to the founding of the Party itself, the First
Revolutionary Civil War (1924–27), the Second Revolutionary War (1927–
37), the Anti-Japanese War of Resistance (1937–45) and the Third Civil War
(1945–49). The photographic accounts of this tumultuous period are of particular interest.

Museum of Chinese History

Occupying two floors of the south (right) wing, this permanent exhibition, though badly lit and with Chinese-language captions only, is a most extensive survey of the evolution of Chinese history and culture. Many of the 10,000 items are replicas or copies of objects belonging to provincial museums around the country which are included as an aid to wider understanding. It is chronologically divided into four sections.

The Primitive Society section exhibits fossils from the Paleolithic, Mesolithic and Neolithic eras. Pottery and bronzes illustrate the Shang and Zhou Dynasties. From the Warring States period on through to the early Qing Dynasty, fabrics, jewellery, lacquerware, porcelain and weaponry have been assembled to show China's scientific and cultural development. The last section covers the period 1840–1919, with exhibits of cannon, weapons, clothing, flags and manuscripts.

Beijing Art Museum

The first major museum to open in Beijing for nearly 30 years, the Beijing Art Museum occupies the grounds of Wanshou Temple (Temple of Longevity) which for years had been occupied by the military. The museum is located immediately off Xisanhuanbeilu (the Third West Ring Road) where it crosses over the canal some 500 metres (1,650 feet) north of the Shangri-La Hotel. Hours are 9 am to 4 pm. The museum is closed on Mondays.

The Wanshou Temple dates back to 1577, when the Ming Wanli emperor erected it on this spot as a library for Buddhist scriptures. In front of the museum runs a canal dug by the Qianlong emperor in the 17th century used by the court to travel by barge from the Forbidden City to the summer palaces in the northwestern suburbs. On the occasion of the 70th birthday of Qianlong's mother, 1,000 Buddhist monks stood on the banks of the canal as part of the birthday celebrations taking place in the temple.

Empress Dowager Cixi stayed in the western section of the temple (soon to be restored) when she broke up her journeys to the Summer Palace. She carried out a major rebuilding campaign in 1894.

The museum has speciality collections of Ming and Qing textiles, Qing and Republican period paintings, Buddhist art, personal name seals Ming and Qing ceramics, and Japanese paintings acquired from collections in the formerly Japanese-occupied areas of Manchuria. The collection was assembled in the late 1980s under the aegis of the Beijing Municipal Bureau of Cultural Relics. Opening times are from 9 am to 4 pm. Closed Monday.

The High Life

HEN his Majesty holds a grand and public court, those who attend it are seated in the following order. The table of the sovereign is placed on an elevation, and he takes his seat on the northern side, with his face turned towards the south; and next to him, on his left hand, sits the Empress. On his right hand are placed his sons, grandsons, and other persons connected with him by blood, upon seats somewhat lower, so that their heads are on a level with the Emperor's feet. The other princes and the nobility have their places at still lower tables; and the same rules are observed with respect to the females, the wives of the sons, grandsons, and other relatives of the Great Khan being seated on the left hand, at tables in like manner gradually lower; then follow the wives of the nobility and military officers: so that all are seated according to their respective ranks and dignities, in the places assigned to them, and to which they are entitled.

The tables are arranged in such a manner that the Great Khan, sitting on his elevated throne, can overlook the whole. It is not, however, to be understood that all who assemble on such occasions can be accommodated at tables. The greater part of the officers, and even of the nobles, on the contrary, eat, sitting upon carpets, in the halls; and on the outside stand a great multitude of persons who come from different countries, and bring with them many rare curiosities.

In the middle of the hall, where the Great Khan sits at table, there is a magnificent piece of furniture, made in the form of a square coffer, each side of which is three paces in length, exquisitely carved in figures of animals, and gilt. It is hollow within, for the purpose of receiving a capacious vase, of pure gold, calculated to hold many gallons. On each of its four sides stands a smaller vessel, containing about a hogshead, one of which is filled with mare's milk, another with that of the camel, and so of the others, according to the kinds of beverage in use. Within this buffet are also the cups or flagons belonging to his Majesty, for serving the liquors. Some of them are of beautiful gilt plate. Their size is such that, when filled with wine or other liquor, the quantity would be sufficient for eight or ten men.

Before every two persons who have seats at the tables, one of these flagons is placed, together with a kind of ladle, in the form of a cup with a handle, also of plate; to be used not only for taking the wine out of the flagon, but for lifting it to the head. This is observed as well with respect to the women as the men. The quantity and richness of the plate belonging to his Majesty is quite incredible.

At each door of the grand hall, or of whatever part the Great Khan happens to be in, stand two officers, of a gigantic figure, one on each side, with staves in their hands, for the purpose of preventing persons from touching the threshold with their feet, and obliging them to step beyond it. If by chance any one is guilty of this offence, these janitors take from him his garment, which he must redeem for money; or, when they do not take the garment, they inflict on him such number of blows as they have authority for doing. But, as strangers may be unacquainted with the prohibition, officers are appointed to introduce and warn them.

The numerous persons who attend at the sideboard of his Majesty, and who serve him with victuals and drink, are all obliged to cover their noses and mouths with handsome veils or cloths of worked silk, in order that his victuals or his wine may not be affected by their breath. When drink is called for by him, and the page in waiting has presented it, he retires three paces and kneels down, upon which the courtiers, and all who are present, in like manner make their prostration. At the same moment all the musical instruments, of which there is a numerous band, begin to play, and continue to do so until he has ceased drinking, when all the company recover their posture. This reverential salutation is made as often as his Majesty drinks. It is unnecessary to say anything of the victuals, because it may well be imagined that their abundance is excessive.

From The Travels of Marco Polo

Lu Xun Museum

This museum in Fuchengmennei Dajie commemorates China's outstanding writer of the 20th century, Lu Xun (1881–1936), who is also noted for his considerable contribution to the liberal movement in China in the 1920s.

The museum, which abuts Lu Xun's former Beijing residence, displays manuscripts, letters, and pages from his personal diary. Some 13,000 books from his library are also in the keeping of the museum, as well as items of clothing and other memorabilia. The museum is open 8.30–11 am and 1.30–4 pm. It is closed on Mondays.

Military Museum of the Chinese People's Revolution

This is a permanent exhibition of 5,000 items—photographs, directives, military uniforms, weaponry and Eighth Route Army insignias, along with portraits of revolutionary heroes and martyrs—covering the Chinese revolutionary army's 29-year history between 1921 and 1949.

The museum is at 9 Fuxing Dajie. Visitors are asked to present their passport for inspection at the entrance. The museum is open 8.30 am–5 pm and closed on Mondays.

Aviation Museum

In 1989, the Chinese Air Force opened this huge display of military and civilian aircraft at Datangshan, Changping County, between Shahe and the Changping county seat, approximately 30 kilometres (19 miles) north of the city limits. After passing through Shahe on the road to Changping, make a right turn at the Baige lu intersection, and watch for the museum on the left. The easiest way to get there is by taxi (tel. 2912457).

The 140 aeroplanes are displayed as in a used car lot. Many are parked outside in long queues, while some 50 choice specimens are housed in a long shed. Military buffs will also enjoy the mobile radar equipment and guided missiles.

Reflecting the history of aviation in China, there are specimens from the Soviet Union, USA and Britain dating back to pre-liberation days, as well as samples of China's own fighting and passenger aircraft.

Exhibits with revolutionary associations include the Ilyushin 12 used to gather samples from a mushroom cloud during a Chinese nuclear test (keep your distance); a Chinese helicopter used by Zhou Enlai during an inspection tour; a single-prop plane that buzzed Tiananmen Square during the celebration of China's first National Day (1 October 1949); a two-engine job that Chairman Mao took to Guangzhou once; and a fighter plane that saw action in the Korean War.

Museum of Natural History

The museum contains four halls devoted to Botany, Zoology, Paleozoology and Paleoanthropology, the latter science being one in which China has contributed much in recent discoveries and research. It is open 8.30 am–5 pm (admission till 4 pm only), and closed on Mondays.

The Temple of Confucius (Kong Miao) and the Former Imperial College (Guozijian)

Situated in Beijing's northeast quarter, close by the Lama Temple, the temple dedicated to Confucius was raised in the Yuan Dynasty and housed the ancestral tablets of Confucius and four other sages. Ceremonials and sacrifices were conducted by the prominent scholars of the day and members of the imperial Court three times a year, including Confucius' birthday.

Part of the temple has been given over to the **Capital Museum**, which exhibits archaeological finds from Beijing and its environs and may be visited between 9 am and 5 pm except on Mondays.

Connected to the museum by a side door is the former **Imperial College** (Guozijian), first built in 1287 and substantially extended in 1784. The focal point of the former college is the square pavilion, which can be thrown open on all four sides by means of doors and shutters, called the Imperial Schoolroom. It is sited in the middle of a pool and reached by bridges. Here the emperor used to lecture on the Classics to ministers and students. On either side of the structure there used to stand 190 stone tablets engraved with 800,000 words of the Thirteen Classics, which took the calligrapher 12 years to transcribe. The tablets have been moved to a courtyard east of the main gate, Taixuemen, and the Imperial College is now the **Capital Library.**

China National Library

The new National Library of China was opened in October 1987. Its total collection of more than 13 million volumes ranks it as the third largest in the world after the Library of Congress in the United States and the Bodleian Library in England. There are many rare books and manuscripts in this collection, some of which date back to the Northern Wei Dynasty (AD 458).

The library is situated on the north side of the Purple Bamboo Garden at Baishiqiao across the road from the Olympic Hotel. The surrounding area is one of the few places in Beijing where there is abundant foliage and scarce traffic or city hustle-bustle. The monolithic appearance of the library's many wings and towers is somewhat mitigated by the soft blue tint of its façade and tea-coloured tile roof which seem to help integrate the building with its surroundings.

If one calls in advance, it is possible to arrange a tour of the library. Foreigners must present their passports at the gate for inspection. The Library is open 8 am–8 pm every day. But visitors are not allowed to enter on Saturdays.

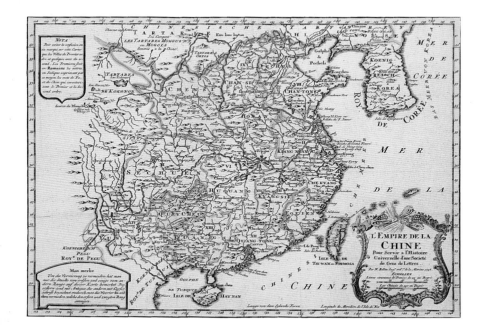

China National Gallery

One cannot help but notice the China National Gallery, a large traditional-style building at the top of Wangfujing. This edifice was constructed in 1959 and is considered one of socialist China's ten best architectural designs. It was entirely refurbished in 1991. The large central building is flanked on either side by long corridors and adjoining wings. Yellow glazed tiles, sloping roofs and upturned eaves lend this building an air of dignity and reserve. There are 14 exhibition rooms and several studios where artists can work.

This gallery holds an increasing number of interesting national and international exhibits and is a good place to discover trends in China's rapidly evolving art world. Many of the works exhibited can be purchased from the artist. Enquiries about how to purchase a painting can be made at the sales shop located in the west wing. The gallery is open everyday until 5 pm, tickets can be purchased until 4.30 pm.

Exhibitions are held from time to time at the **Nationalities Cultural Palace** (Minzu Wenhua Gong), Fuxingmennei Dajie.

Recommended Reading

Oxford University Press in Hong Kong has done a great deed by having made available in affordable hardback and paperback reprints of some of the classic works in English about Beijing. Three indispensible titles that describe the city as it was from the 1920s to 1940s are the highly detailed *In Search of Old Peking* by Arlington and Lewisohn; the more prosaic and evocative *Peking* by Juliet Bredon; and the apotheosis of life in Old Peking, George Kate's *The Years that were Fat: The Last of Old China*. A recent historical walking tour guide to the major sites in the city is *Beijingwalks* (Henry Holt) by Don J Cohn and Zhang Jingqing.

Nagel's *Encyclopedia-Guide to China* has a wealth of historical information about Beijing but is embarrasingly out of date for practical information. A number of attractive coffee-table books published about the capital include the Time-Life volume *Peking*, written by David Bonavia, with excellent photographs by Peter Griffiths, and Leong Ka Tai's photographic essay, *Beijing* (Times Edition Singapore), with a text by Frank Ching, and the earlier *Peking: A Tale of Three Cities*, by Nigel Cameron with memorable photographs of the 1960s by Brian Brake.

There are some books written by foreigners who have lived in Beijing in recent years which offer particular insight into Chinese life and politics. Bernard Frolic's *Mao's People* (Harvard), Simon Ley's *Broken Images* (Allison & Busby) and *Chinese Shadows* (Viking) and David Bonavia's *The Chinese* (Penguin) are highly informative and readable. Ruth Sidel gives a detailed description of the structure of life in a Beijing neighbourhood in her *Families of Fengsheng—Urban Life in China* (Penguin), while Beverley Hooper tells of student life in *Inside Peking* (MacDonald & Jane's). One of the first western journalists to be accredited in the aftermath of the Cultural Revolution, the correspondent of *Der Spiegel* Tizano Terzani, published his experiences in *The Forbidden Door* (Asia 2000 Ltd) after he was expelled from China in 1984.

Two personal accounts of the old days are David Kidd, *Peking Story: The Last Days of Old China* (Clarkson N Potter) and John Blofeld's *City of Lingering Splendour: A Frank Account of Old Peking's Exotic Pleasures* (Hutchinson). Of great historial interest is *Twilight in the Forbidden City* (Oxford reprint) by Reginald Johnston, the English tutor and tennis teacher of Puyi, the last emperor of the Qing dynasty.

Three further literary accounts in the Hong Kong Oxford reprint series are Osbert Sitwell's *Escape with Me!*, Harold Acton's *Peonies and Ponies*, and the surprisingly insightful *Superficial Journey through Tokyo and Peking*.

Other penetrating journalistic coverage, including interesting details about life in Beijing in the 1970s and early 1980s, can be found in *China-Alive in the*

Bitter Sea, by *New York Times* correspondent, Fox Butterfield; *China after Mao—Coming Alive* by British diplomat, Roger Garside; *The Chinese—Portrait of a People*, by the Canadian journalist John Fraser; and *From the Center of the Earth* by Richard Bernstein. The end of the Qing Dynasty is graphically portrayed in two autobiographies—*Two Years in The Forbidden City* by Der Ling, a Manchu princess who was a lady-in-waiting to the Empress Dowager Cixi, and *From Emperor to Citizen* (Beijing Foreign Languages Press) by the last emperor, Puyi. Marina Warner's biography of the Empress Dowager, *The Dragon Empress* (Weidenfeld & Nicolson), is particularly entertaining. The old Qing Summer Palace, Yuanmingyuan, is described in great detail, accompanied by reproductions of contemporary paintings and copperplate etchings, in *Yuanmingyuan* (Joint Publishing), currently available only with a Chinese text. A similar production by the same publisher is *The Architecture of the Forbidden City*.

Those interested in reading some of China's classical novels will enjoy *Dream of the Red Chamber* by the 18th-century novelist Cao Xueqin—translated as *The Story of the Stone* by David Hawkes and John Minford (5 volumes, Penguin) or as *A Dream of Red Mansions* (3 volumes, Beijing Foreign Languages Press), rendered into English by Yang Hsien-yi and Gladys Yang. A garden featured in the novel—*Daguanyuan*—has been recreated as a park in the southwest of Beijing.

Life in pre-revolutionary China is vividly portrayed in *Rickshaw: The Novel of Luotuo Xiangzi* by Lao She (University Press of Hawaii), and *Family* by Ba Jin (Doubleday)— both well worth reading. The *Selected Stories of Lu Xun*, China's best-loved 20th-century writer, is translated by Yang Hsien-yi and Gladys Yang for Beijing Foreign Languages Press.

Two wonderful titles that treat the customs and folkways of Old Peking are *Annual Customs and Festivals in Peking* (Hong Kong University Press), translated and annotated by Derk Bodde, and the utterly charming *The Adventures of Wu: The Life Cycle of a Peking Man* (Princeton University Press) by H Y Lowe, a Chinese journalist of the 1930s.

A contemporary poet and writer of fiction who has been hailed as a new voice in the post-Cultural Revolution literary scene is Beijing-born Zhao Zhenkai (pen-name Bei Dao), whose collection of short stories, *Waves*, has been translated by Bonnie S McDougall and Susette Ternent Cooke (The Chinese University Press, Hong Kong). *Seeds of Fire: Chinese Voices of Conscience* edited by Geremie Barmé and John Minford, is an anthology of writings— poetry, essays and extracts from novels—representing the new 'literature of conscience'. It is published by Farrar, Straus and Giroux, New York.

For a good picture of life in the foreign community in Beijing in the 1920s read Ann Bridge's novel *Peking Picnic* (Triad Granada). Oxford University

Press's *A Photographer in Old Peking* is a beautiful volume of rare black-and-white photographs taken between 1933 and 1946, interspersed with an evocative account of people and places by the photographer Hedda Morrison. The tale of a great eccentric is told by historian Hugh Trevor-Roper in *Hermit of Peking: The Hidden Life of Sir Edmund Backhouse*.

Hong Kong University Press has published a comprehensive book on *The Ming Tombs*, written by Anne Paludan. A much reduced version of the same book has been published by Oxford in Hong Kong.

For those with a special interest in the subject, Elizabeth Halston's *Peking Opera* (Oxford University Press) is one of the best books in English. A concise paperback on the subject appeared in 1981 in Beijing—*Peking Opera and Mei Lanfang: a Guide to China's Traditional Theatre and the Arts of its Great Master* by Wu Zuguang, Huang Zuolin and Mei Shaowu (New World Press). *Mei Lanfang—Leader of the Pear Garden* by A. C Scott is written with much absorbing background (Hong Kong University Press). For general histories of China, a little known gem is *A Short History of the Chinese People* (Harper) by L Carrington Goodrich, which brings up to the early 20th century. Slightly longer is Jacques Gernet's *A History of Chinese Civilization* (Cambridge). Modern China is well covered in Jonathan Spence's *The Search for Modern China* (W W Norton), and *The Rise of Modern China* by Immanuel Hsu (Oxford).

Practical Information

Hotels

Over the past few years there has been a rapid surge of hotel construction in Beijing in an attempt to keep pace with demand from the fast-increasing number of visitors who flock to the capital. Beijing's hotels offer the visitor quite a choice of quality and price, ranging from the upmarket Shangri-La or Park Hotel, down to utilitarian hostelries where you may stay, dormitory-style, for a few *yuan*. Quality of management covers an equally broad spectrum. In some hotels you will find polite, well-intentioned (possibly well-trained) English-speaking staff; in others, management still pays little attention to cleanliness, maintenance, or charm.

Beijing Municipality lists over 200 hotels in the city which accept overseas guests. In practice some of these are not keen to have foreigners stay there. The reasons for this include problems with language, inflexible meal times, unreliable hot water supply etc. Others could only be recommended as a last resort when everywhere else in the city is full.

Beijing's top hotels are mostly financed from overseas and run by foreign management groups. With overseas staff (many are from Hong Kong) in top managerial positions, these joint-venture hotels are aiming at international standard service and facilities—and they charge international price for them.

The new joint-venture hotels have the great advantage of a workable confirmed booking system—always a major difficulty for non-group travellers in China. As a rule, it is difficult to get confirmed bookings for Beijing's Chinese-run hotels, even though more travel agencies, including CITS, can now arrrange bookings for a select few. Attempts by individuals to get bookings confirmed by letter or telex still tend to go unanswered.

In peak months (March through to November), rooms in the capital have been very hard to come by. Although the shortage should ease as more hotels open up over the next few years, it is still advisable for travellers who want a good hotel to book it as far in advance as possible.

Some of Beijing's older hotels, run by the municipality, have been inspired by standards set by new hotels, and have made visible efforts to improve—though none seem entirely able to throw off the quirks of hotel management Chinese-style.

Chinese-run hotels typically have private bathroom, telephone, heating, and sometimes air-conditioning. Boiled drinking water is placed in each room. There are outlets for electric razors, the current being 220 volts. There are TV sets in the public lounges and sometimes in rooms. Room service is patchy, but one can usually get beer and soft drinks until late at night by approaching the floor-attendants who look after most services. There are small shops, bank, postal and telegraph facilities in the hotel foyers. Chinese and western food is available, and private dinner parties and banquets can be arranged. Standard meal charges will be in the range of Rmb50 per day, exclusive of drinks and special dishes. A range of imported foreign wines and spirits, Coca-Cola, cigarettes and films can be bought at special stalls in most big hotels and Friendship Stores. Some hotels also stock overseas newspapers and magazines.

In many Chinese hotels, the attendants have an irritating habit of opening the door one has carefully locked. Try not to be annoyed—they are confident that no-one is going to interfere with our possessions. But be prepared for attendants walking into your room with barely a knock, and even dusting around while you are trying to change. Do bear in mind that thefts may occur in budget hotels.

The following list of hotels gives an approximate range of rates for rooms and suites in mid-1991, to be used as a basis for comparison, rather than an accurate picture of current prices many of which are discounted from 15 to 50 percent. Only special facilities (beyond TV, bank, post office, hairdresser, tourist shops) have been mentioned. Note that hotels in Beijing now add a 15 percent service charge to the room rate.

H.S.B.C. Peking Staff 1925
Seated (Left to Right) –

Superior

Beijing Hotel 北京饭店 东长安街 3号
33 Dongchang'an Dajie. Tel. 5137766; tlx. 22426; cable 6531; fax.5137307

910 rooms, Rmb228–1,040. Business centre, conference and banqueting hall (max. 1,000). Beijing's oldest (1900) and best known hotel. Centrally located near Tiananmen Square. This hotel has character but its age is apparent.

China World Hotel 中国大饭店 建国门外大街 1 号
1 Jianguomenwai Dajie. Tel. 5052266; tlx. 211206; fax. 5053167

743 rooms, US$150–1200. Health club, gym, sauna, swimming pool, night-club/disco, supermarket, conference and banquet facilities (max. 2000), Jewel in the crown of the Shangri-La hotels in China, this hotel is part of a huge new complex that includes the Traders Hotel and the China World Trade Center, thus offering every conceivable service. There are over 20 restaurants and bars.

Diaoyutai State Guesthouse 钓鱼台国宾馆 三里河路
(Angler's State Guesthouse) Sanlihe Lu. Tel. 8031188; tlx. 22798; fax. 8013362

Rooms from US$140. Extensive gardens, lake (fishing and boating. Set in a very attractive wooded parkland. Several buildings are made available to foreign tour groups with sufficient numbers of guests.

Dragon Spring Mövenpick-Radisson Guesthouse 龙泉宾馆 门头沟水池北路
Shuichi Bei Lu, Mentougou. Tel. 9843362; tlx. 222292/3; fax. 3014377

235 rooms and suites, US$70–140, conference (max. 500) and banqueting (max. 180) facilities, indoor pool, tennis courts, health club, billiard room, secretarial services. Traditional Chinese architecture; pleasant atmosphere. A joint-venture hotel, very remotely located near the Fragrant Hills. Boasts of having the best ice cream in Beijing. Shuttle service to city centre.

Grand Hotel Beijing 北京贵宾楼饭店 东长安街35号
35 Dong Chang'an Jie. Tel. 5137788; tlx. 210617–8; fax. 5130049–50

218 rooms and suites, US$150–280, business centre, health club. Westernmost wing of the Beijing Hotel, but independently managed. Large atrium, Chinese style decor, fine location, intimate comfort.

Great Wall Sheraton
Donghuan Bei Lu, Chaoyang. Tel. 5005566; tlx. 22002, 20045; fax. 5001938

1,007 rooms, US$110–860, executive floor, 24-hour business centre, nightclub, Clark Hatch health centre, indoor/outdoor swimming pool, tennis, billiards, theatre (max. 900), ballroom (max. 1,800), conference and banquet (max. 1,000). (Amex, Diners, Visa, Mastercharge, Federal, Great Wall Card.) Very convenient, plush interior; joint-venture hotel located near Sanlitun embassy district. Shuttle service to city centre.

Holiday Inn Lido Beijing
Jichang Lu, Jiangtai Lu. Tel. 5006688; tlx. 22618; fax. 5006237

1,000 rooms, US$120–520, health club, bowling centre, indoor swimming pool, billiards, TV games, supermarket, delicatessen, disco. (Amex Diners, Visa, Mastercharge.) Very remote location, but close to the airport; offers the widest range of facilities including a sports club. Joint-venture hotel. Shuttle service to city centre.

Jianguo
Jianguomenwai Dajie. Tel. 5002233; tlx. 22439; fax. 5002871

457 rooms, US$115–215, ballroom (max. 200), indoor swimming pool, delicatessen. (Visa, Diners, Amex.) Within walking distance of major business centres in Beijing, pleasant atmosphere; joint-venture hotel. Favoured by long time visitors.

Jinglun (Beijing-Toronto)
Jianguomenwai Dajie. Tel. 5002266; tlx. 210012; cable 5650; fax. 5002022

695 rooms, US$100-190, business centre, ballroom (max. 400). (Visa, Mastercharge.) Within walking distance of major business centres, very efficient service; joint-venture hotel.

The Palace Hotel
Wangfujing. Tel. 5128899; tlx. 222696; fax. 5129050

575 rooms, US$120–1,500, business centre, indoor swimming pool, health club, disco, billiards, delicatessen, western, Chinese and Japanese restaurants, conference (max. 550) and banquet (max. 400) facilities. Stunning luxury hotel in fine location. Managed by the Peninsula Group of Hong Kong in snappy Hong Kong style.

China's imperial past lived again in 1986 when Italian director Bernardo Bertolucci shot his epic The Last Emperor *within the walls of the Forbidden City.*

Shangri-La 香格里拉饭店　紫竹院路29号
29 Zizhuyan Lu. Tel. 8412211; tlx. 222322; fax. 8418006

786 rooms, US$100-720, business centre, health club and indoor swimming pool, music room, ballroom and function rooms (max. 750). (Amex, Visa, Mastercharge.) Elegant, comfortable; a joint-venture hotel, a bit remote. Shuttle service to the city centre. The Horizon Floor executive rooms here are some of the nicest in the city.

Swissotel, Hong Kong Macau Centre 北京港澳中心　朝阳门北大街工人体育场北路
Gongren tiyuchangbei Lu, Chaoyang District. Tel. 5012288; tlx. 222527; fax. 5012501

500 rooms, US$110–230, Health club, indoor swimming pool, tennis court, office and residential tower, convention and meeting facilities (banquet max. 400). First hotel in Asia with full facilities for the handicapped. In a large commercial and hotel complex, this is the only hotel in China that offers members of the Hong Kong Jockey Club off track betting at the Happy Valley Race Course in Hong Kong.

Tianlun Dynasty Hotel 北京天伦王朝饭店　王府井大街50号
50 Wangfujing Dajie. Tel. 5138888; tlx. 210575; fax. 5137866

408 rooms, US$120–3,000, business centre, bowling alley, tennis and squash courts available, disco, rooftop garden, Vietnamese restaurant, conference and

The film documents Pu Yi's short-lived reign from the age of three, the ill-fated 'restoration' as puppet emperor of Manchukuo, and his final days as a simple gardener in Beijing

banquet facilities (max. 600). Opened 1991. Luxury hotel featuring the largest atrium in East Asia. Excellent downtown location.

Tianping Lee Gardens Hotel 天平利园酒店　北京建国门南大街 2 号
2 Jianguomennan Dajie. Tel. 5138855; fax. 5120619

430 rooms, US$100–800, business centre, indoor swimming pool, sauna, gymnasium, Lawyers Club (pub, library, offices), conference and banquet facilities, (max. 350). Located near the Friendship Store in the embassy
district. Well run upmarket hotel under Hong Kong ownership and manage-ment.

First Class
Beijing Airport Mövenpick Radisson Hotel 北京国都大饭店　首都机场南小天竺路
Xiao Tianzhu Village, Shunyi County. Tel. 4565588; fax. 4565678

420 rooms, US$110–125, 24-hour business centre, outdoor tennis courts, indoor pool, gym, pub. Five minutes from the airport but 40 minutes from town. Excellent food services, including arguably the best ice cream in China.

Beijing International Hotel 北京国际饭店　建国门内大街 9 号
9 Jianguomennei Dajie. Tel. 5126688; tlx. 211121; fax. 5129972

1,049 rooms and suites, US$120–200, business centre, health centre, tennis courts, indoor/outdoor pool, bowling centre, billiards, game room shopping arcade. A massive structure built by the Chinese International Travel Service. It is a five-minute taxi ride to Tiananmen Square and near the Beijing train station. Staff friendly, but telling reminders that this hotel is run entirely under Chinese management.

Chang Fu Gong New Otani Hotel 长富宫饭店   建国门外大街
Jianguomenwai Dajie. Tel. 5125555; tlx. 222936; fax. 5125346

512 rooms, US$110–400, grand ballroom, Japanese restaurant, health club, indoor pool, tennis courts, sauna, banquet and conference facilities (max. 700). Large Japanese-managed hotel that handles many Japanese tour groups. Located near the Friendship Store in the embassy district.

Exhibition Centre Hotel 北京展览馆宾馆   西直门外大街135号
135 Xizhimenwai Dajie. Tel. 8316633; cable 1717; fax. 8327450

250 rooms, US$85–130, health club, American pub. Friendly, upbeat, well managed joint venture, near the Beijing Zoo on the grounds of the Russian-built exhibition centre.

Fragrant Hills (Xiangshan) Hotel 香山饭店   香山
Xiangshan. Tel. 2565544; tlx. 222202 FHCM; cable 7391; fax. 2566794

288 rooms, Rmb210–1,380, health club, outdoor pool, tennis, gardens. Designed by I M Pei; a striking location in Fragrant Hills Park. Facilities suffering from neglect; very remote from the city's centre.

Holiday Inn Downtown 北京金都假日饭店   西城区北礼士路98号
98 Beilishi Lu. Tel. 8322288; tlx. 221045; fax. 8064696

347 rooms, US$85–335, swimming pool, health club, Indian restaurant. Opened in 1990. Economical, unpretentious hotel in a non-tourist neighbourhood.

Jing Guang New World Hotel 京广新世界饭店   朝阳区呼家楼
Hu Jia Lou, Chaoyang District. Tel. 5018888; tlx. 210489; fax. 5013333

492 rooms, US$110–450, medical clinic, taxi fleet, supermarket, disco, Chaozhou restaurant, Food Street. In a commercial and residential skyscraper somewhat outside the city centre.

Kunlun Hotel 昆仑饭店　朝日亮马桥21号
21 Liangmaqiao, Chaoyang. Tel. 5003388; tlx. 210327; fax. 5003228

1,005 rooms, US$110–1000, health club, swimming pool (indoor), tennis courts, nightclub, ballroom and conference facilities (max. 120). Located near Sanlitun embassy district; good facilities but inconsistent service.

Landmark Hotel 亮马饭店（亮马公寓）　北三环路 8 号
8 Beisanhuan Lu. Tel. 5016688; tlx. 210301; fax. 5013513

500 rooms, US$65–200, medical clinic, baby-sitting, drug store, courier service, indoor swimming pool, sauna, tennis and squash court, health club, conference and banquet facilities (max. 50). Opened 1990. Residential and commercial complex a stone's throw from the Sheraton Great Wall near the diplomatic quarter. Joint venture with Hong Kong and Singapore, run by Beijing Travel and Tourism Corporation.

Meridien Jin Lang Hotel 北京金朗大酒店　东城区崇内大街75号
75 Chongnei Dajie. Tel. 5132288; fax. 5125839

408 rooms, US$75–450, French brasserie, health club, business centre, conference and banquet facilities (max. 110). Air France hotel, convenient downtown location near Beijing Train Station and historical neighbourhoods.

Ming Yuan Hotel 明苑宾馆　十三陵
Shisanling. P O Box: 1003, Beijing. Tel. 9746831; tlx. 222486
Changping 6831, tlx. 222486

105 rooms, FEC100–280. Most major facilities. Scenic setting outside Beijing near Ming tombs and Great Wall.

Olympic Hotel 奥林匹克饭店　海淀区白石桥路25号（首都体育馆北首）
52 Baishiqiao Lu. Tel. 8316688; tlx. 222749; fax. 8318390

338 rooms, US$95–400, business centre, shop, French restaurant, Cantonese restaurant, two bars, 24-hour coffee shop, hair salon, Chinese medical centre, conference facilities (max. 300), shuttle service to city centre. Hotel is located in pleasant surroundings near Purple Bamboo Park and Capital Gymnasium. A joint-venture hotel; attractive, cheery.

Traders Hotel 国贸饭店（国贸中心）　建国门外大街 1 号
1 Jianguomenwai Dajie. Tel. 5052277; tlx. 222981; fax. 5050818, 5050828

298 rooms, US$100–175, access to China World Hotel facilities. Younger sibling of the China World Hotel, the Traders is a modest, well-run hotel favoured by businessmen.

Xin Da Du Hotel 新大都饭店　西城区车公庄大街21号
21 Chegongzhuang Road. Tel. 8319988; tlx. 221042–3; fax. 8322135–6

400 rooms, US$80–170. Business centre, bowling alley. Beautifully renovated tourist hotel run by Beijing Municipality. Located in a residential area near the Beijing Zoo.

Xiyuan Hotel 西苑饭店　二星沟
Erligou. Tel. 8313388; tlx. 2283; cable 8766; fax. 8314577

750 rooms, US$45–258, health club, indoor swimming pool, business centre. Good facilities but inadequate service. Located near Erligou, Negotiations Building and Beijing Zoo.

Zhaolong Hotel 兆龙饭店　朝阳工人体育场北路
2 Gongren Tiyuchang Bei Lu, Chaoyang. Tel. 5002299; tlx. 210079; fax. 5003319

270 rooms, US$73, theatre (max. 200), banquet (max. 300), health club, indoor/

outdoor pool. This hotel was a gift to China from Hong Kong shipping magnate Y K Pao. Located near Jianguomenwai business area. Hotel standards have suffered under Chinese management.

A number of additional first class hotels opened in 1991. They include the **Holiday Inn Crowne Plaza**, 38 Wangfujing Dajie. Holiday Inn's third Beijing hotel; **SAS Royal Hotel**, near the China International Exhibition Center in the Chaoyang district, and the **Sara Hotel Beijing (Hua Qiao Da Sha)**, a Swedish joint venture built on the sight of the former Overseas Chinese Mansion on Wangfujing.

Standard
Beijing Tianyuanzhuang Hotel
Yuanmingyuan Xi Lu. Tel. 289661

154 rooms, Rmb120–280, Chinese restaurant, western restaurant, bar, cafe, shop. In the north of the city situated near orchards and nurseries. One outstanding feature of this hotel is a nearby fishing pond from which guests can catch fish and have their catch prepared by the hotel's chef.

Capital Hotel
3 Qianmen Dong Dajie. Tel. 5129988; tlx. 222650; cable 6172; fax. 5120323

296 rooms, Rmb90–400, business centre, western restaurant, Chinese restaurant, Japanese restaurant, coffee shop, bar, shopping arcade, swimming pool, tennis courts, bowling alley, billiards, sauna and steam room, conference and banquet facilities (max. 400). Centrally located in a busy section of town. Owned by the State Council displays some Chinese characteristics.

Huado
8 Xinyuan Nan Lu. Tel. 5001166; tlx. 22028; cable 5431; fax. 5001615

522 rooms, Rmb130–260, ballroom and conference facilities (max. 500), banquet (max. 50). Built and run by CTS. Few taxis and no buses make it an inconvenient place to stay.

Friendship Hotel
3 Baishiqiao Lu. Tel. 8498888; tlx. 22362; cable 2222; fax 8314661

1,500 rooms, Rmb120–280, outdoor swimming pool, gymnasium, theatre, tennis courts. Originally built to house Russian experts in the 50s, it is a massive complex of many buildings. Pleasant atmosphere. Shuttle service to city centre.

Clutching at Straws

igh on the *Venerable Schoolmaster Gao's list of gripes was the gall of the man who had edited* A General Textbook of Chinese History *in not taking the classroom teacher into account when putting this text together. Though some of it did tally with* Liaofan's Shorter History, *there were large chunks that didn't, so that it was impossible to weave the two books together into any kind of coherent lecture. The Venerable Schoolmaster Gao glanced at a slip of paper that had been left in the textbook, and his smouldering resentment against the teacher who had quit halfway through the course was fanned into a full blaze, for the note read:* Begin at Chapter Eight—The Rise and Fall of the Eastern Jin Dyansty [317–420]. *If that clod hadn't already finished lecturing on the Three Kingdoms Period [220–65], Gao himself wouldn't have had nearly so much difficulty preparing. He knew the Three Kingdoms Period up one side and down the other:* The Triple Oath of the Peach Garden, Kong Ming Borrows Arrows, Zhou Yü Thrice Angered, Huang Zhong Beheads Xia Houyuan at Dingjun Mountain, *and any number of other such incidents.* [1]

And if it had only been some later period—let's say the Tang Dynasty [618–907]—well, then you had material like Qin Qiong Sells His Horse.[2] *Yes, he could have told stories like that in a pretty entertaining way, too. But no! It couldn't be the Three Kingdoms or the Tang, it had to be that damned Eastern Jing right in between! Once more, Gao sighed in exasperation; and once more too, he made a dive for* Liaofan's Shorter History.

1. *All of these episodes are contained in the popular historical novel* Romance of the Three Kingdoms. *In a Western setting, a character like Gao might consider familiarity with Dickens'* Tale of Two Cities *and Hugo's* Ninety-three *sufficient qualification for offering a course on the French Revolution.*

2. *Qin Qiong was a military hero who helped the first Tang emperor found the new dynasty. Again, Gao's knowledge is derived from popular fiction.*

Lu Xun, 'The Venerable Schoolmaster Gao',
translated by William A Lyell

Minzu 民族饭店　复兴门内大街51号
51 Fuxingmennei Dajie. Tel. 6014466; tlx. 200912; cable 8541; fax. 6014849

615 rooms, FEC175–195, conference and banquet facilities (max. 400), gym, billiards. Recently renovated. Located on west side of Tiananmen Square near Xidan street. An important shopping area.

New World Tower 新世界宾馆　朝阳区工体东路 4 号
4 Gongren Tiyuchangdong Lu. Tel. 5007799; tlx. 210530; fax. 5007668

85 rooms, 135 studios and suites, US$60–135, business centre, nursery, karaoke, health club. Not to be confused with Jing Guang New World Hotel, this is a modest slightly run down hotel near the Sanlitun diplomatic district.

Park Hotel 北京百牙酒店　浦黄榆路36号
36 Puhuangyu Lu. Tel. 7212233; tlx. 22968; cable 8877; fax 7211615

140 rooms, Rmb190–320, business centre, clinic, disco, Sichuan restaurant, western restaurant, Korean restaurant, shuttle service to city centre. A joint-venture hotel. This hotel has good facilities and an attractive interior. The exterior and surrounding area is less than desirable. Located in an underdeveloped section of Beijing, south of Tiantan Park.

Qianmen 前门饭店　永安路 1 号
1 Yongan Lu. Tel. 3016688; tlx. 222382; fax. 3013883

460 rooms, Rmb172–400. Located in an interesting old section of Beijing near Liulichang (Beijing's best known antiques street). Service is adequate. Nightly Beijing opera performances are given in the Liyuan (Pear Garden) Theatre.

Ramada Asia Hotel 北京华美达亚洲大酒店　中国北京工体北路新中西街 8 号
8 Xinzhongxi Lu, Gongtibei Lu. Tel. 5007788; tlx. 2110597; fax. 5008091

298 rooms and suites, US$120–600, health club, Chinese Mediterranean and Korean restaurants, pizza and pasta restaurant. Opened in 1990 with a plethora of infrastructure problems, particularly a poor construction job. Best to avoid until things are straightened out.

Taiwan Hotel 台湾饭店　王府井北金鱼胡同 5 号
5 Jinyu Hutong. Tel. 5136688; tlx. 210543; fax. 51136898

268 rooms, US$80–250, business centre, health club. Well located near

Wangfujing (and the Palace Hotel). Inexpensive tourist hotel that offers concessions to groups from Taiwan.

Xinqiao 新桥饭店　崇文门东交民巷 2 号
2 Dongjiaomin Xiang, Chongwenmen. Tel. 557731

320 rooms, Rmb205–360, conference and banquet facilities (max. 300), health centre, boulangerie. Located in old Legation Quarter near the centre of the city. Renovated in 1991.

Yanjing 燕京宾馆　复兴门外大街 2 号
2 Fuxingmenwai Dajie. Tel. 8326611; tlx 20028; cable 5046; fax. 8326130

507 rooms, Rmb115–220. A rather cheerless building with few facilities. Most guests are long-term businessmen.

Yanxiang 燕翔饭店　将台路 2 号
2 Jiangtai Lu. Tel. 5006666; tlx. 210014; cable 1500; fax. 5006231

515 rooms, Rmb200–400, ballroom (max. 150), banquet facilities (max. 300), indoor swimming pool. Very remote; next door to Holiday Inn Lido; mainly used by tourist groups.

Youhao Binguan 友好宾馆　交道口后园恩寺 7 号
7 Houyuanensi, Jiaodaokou. Tel. 441036

50 rooms, Rmb100–300. Charming atmosphere—former residence of Chiang Kai-Shek. Reputed to have the best Japanese restaurant in Beijing.

Zhuyuan Guesthouse 竹园宾馆　阳鼓楼大街小石桥胡同24号
24 Xiaoshiqiao Hutong, Jiugulou Dajie. Tel. 444661; cable 3428

39 rooms, Rmb80–380. Picturesque setting with covered walkways and gardens. The hotel is the former residence of Kong Sheng, head of the Public Security Bureau during the Cultural Revolution. Difficult to get reservations.

Zijing Binguan 紫金宾馆　崇文门西大街 9 号
(formerly Guesthouse number 14) 9 Chongwenmen Xi Dajie. Tel. 5136655

17 rooms, Rmb260–350 full board. This is a small, centrally located hotel. Primarily used by long-term businessmen.

Budget Hotels

Beiwei 北纬饭店   北纬路13号
13 Xijing Lu. Tel. 3012266

226 rooms, Rmb140–221. Adequate facilities, friendly service. Located near Qianmen shopping district.

Guanghua 光华饭店   东环中路38号
38 Donghuan Zhong Lu. Tel. 5018866

204 room, Rmb150. Simple, clean, friendly; a bit inconvenient.

Hadamen Hotel 哈德门饭店   崇文门外大街甲 2 号
2A Chongwenmenwai Dajie. Tel. 7012244; tlx. 210337; cable 7573; fax. 7016865

210 rooms, Rmb128–210, business centre, Bianyifang Peking Roast Duck Restaurant. Near the Beijing Railway Station, this is a conveniently located basic hotel.

Huguosi Hotel 护国寺饭店 西城区护国寺街
Huguosi Jie, Western District. Tel. 6011113; tlx. 222958; fax. 6012335

80 rooms, Rmb80–90, coffee shop, Chinese restaurants. Located in the heart of the old city on a bustling street.

Huilongguan 汇龙观 德胜门外
Deshengmenwai. Tel. 275931

350 rooms, Rmb86–100. Reasonable facilities; transportation is a problem.

Huizhong Hotel 惠中饭店 珠市口西大街120号
120 Zhushikou Xi Dajie. Tel. 3012255; tlx. 222693

300 rooms, Rmb42–150. Near Qianmen shopping district; good facilities and service.

Jimen Hotel 蓟门饭店 海淀区学院路1号
1 Xueyuan Lu. Tel. 2016701; tlx. 222325; cable 5636; fax. 2015355

200 rooms, Rmb66–120, Chinese restaurant, bar. A spartan building with adequate facilities and service. It is rather isolated in the northwest of Beijing but convenient to Beijing University, Qinghua University and Beijing Languages Institute.

Longxiang Hotel 龙翔饭店 海淀区龙翔路15号
15 Longxiang Lu. Tel. 2013355; tlx. 222590; fax. 2015595

234 rooms, Rmb80–138, business centre, shop, disco, coffee shop, tea room, Chinese restaurant, western restaurant. The facilities are adequate if unexciting. Its isolated location on a lonely road in the north of Beijing makes transportation difficult.

Nanhua 南华饭店 宣武区虎坊路南华西路11号
11 Nanhua Xi Lu, Hufang Lu, Xuanwu. Tel. 3022221; cable 7916

50 rooms, Rmb100–180. Located in a small *hutong* near the Qianmen Hotel, this small new hotel has friendly staff who welcome foreign guests.

Safe and Sound

As for the good Government, Quietness and Ease and Cleanliness of the Jail, I do not question but it exceeds ours in Europe. As soon as we were brought into the First Court we spy'd the Head Jailor, who sat in great State on his Tribunal-seat; he presently ask'd for the 'mittimus' of the Criminal Judg that had sent us to him. But him we had not yet seen, (for he was still not come to himself after a great Feast he had been at the day before) so one of his Deputies sent us to Prison. Then the Goaler began to examine us concerning our coming to China, upon what intent it was, what we liv'd upon, &c. We answer'd him with a great deal of freedom and ease, the Consequence whereof was that they put us in through another little Door which was lock'd, and had a Porter at it; we went on through a Lane, and they brought us to an Idol Temple. I dont know that in the Prisons in these our Countries there is any Church of God so great, so spacious, so clean, so neat, and so much frequented by the Prisoners as that is. In all the Goals, Dungeons and Courts of Justice throughout the Empire, they have Temples richly adorn'd, and cleanly, where the Prisoners, and such as have law-suits make their Suits; but, those Wooden and Earthen Images neither hearing nor seeing, they give no Relief to their Suppliants. At Night they turn'd us through another Lesser Door into a Court, and then convey'd us into a great Hall, quite dark and dismal, without any Window and so full of People, that there was hardly room for them to stand; this was call'd the little Prison to distinguish it from the Dungeon which was far enough from thence. Here we continued 40 days, having always Light at night and there was an Over seer who took care no Noise should be made. All Men were wonderful submissive to him, so that there was no roaring, or noise, or quarrelling, but all as hush'd as if it had been the Novice-house of a well govern'd Monastery, which we did not a little admire.

The Travels and Controversies of
Friar Domingo Navarrete, *1618–1686*

Overseas Chinese Hotel (Huaqiao Binguan) 华侨宾馆　北新桥三条5号
5 Santiao Beixinqiao. Tel. 4016688
175 rooms, Rmb120–190. Near the Lama temple in north of city, transportation is difficult to arrange.

Parkview Tiantan Hotel 天坛饭店　崇文区体育馆路1号
1 Tiyuguan Road, Chongwen District. Tel. 7012277; tlx. 221034; fax. 7016833

200 rooms, Rmb170.

Qiaoyuan 侨园饭店　右安门外东宾河路
Youanmenwai, Dongbinhe Lu. Tel. 338861

200 rooms, Rmb8 (dormitory)–Rmb32. A budget hotel; pleasant, if inconveniently located.

Tiantan Tiyu Binguan (Sportsmen's Inn) 天坛体育宾馆　体育馆路10号
10 Tiyuguan Lu. Tel. 7013388; tlx. 22238; cable 3128; fax. 7015388

100 rooms, Rmb68–100. Few buses or taxis; good facilities, pleasant staff.

Wanshou 万寿宾馆　万寿路12A号
12A Wanshou Lu. Tel. 8214433; tlx. 222873; cable 6102; fax. 8216290

80 rooms, Rmb70–170. Adequate facilities, interesting neighbourhood.

Ziyu 紫玉饭店　西三环北路花园村5号
5 Huayuancun, Xisanhuan Bei Lu. Tel. 890191; tlx. 22078; cable 6994
125 rooms, Rmb50–110.

Recommended Restaurants

Most Chinese restaurants in the west serve Cantonese, Sichuan or Shanghai food. The typical food of Beijing is rather different. Rice is not grown in north China as abundantly as in the south and the staple cereal is wheat. Steamed bread, dumplings and many kinds of noodles form the basis of any Beijing meal. The most commonly eaten vegetables are those of a northern climate—carrots, spinach, turnips, onions, scallions, and large white cabbages.

Beijing has adopted and modified various northern cooking techniques—particularly for barbecueing or boiling mutton—which are not a special feature of its cuisine. But the capital's most celebrated dish, famous far beyond the borders of China, is Peking duck (pardon us for retaining the old spelling).

White-feathered Beijing ducks are raised in the outskirts of the city. One such farm, near Landianchang alongside the Jingma Irrigation Canal that flows out of Kunming Lake, can be visited on the way to the Summer Palace. For the last two weeks of their life, the ducks are force fed a rich diet of grain and beans. When they reach the kitchen, boiling water is poured over the bird, which is then hung for several hours to dry. The duck is basted with syrup, and air is pumped into it to separate the skin from the layer of fat underneath, so ensuring that the skin is crisped while the bird cooks on a spit. The skin, which is the delicacy, is eaten with small pancakes, scallions and a thick, salty bean, sauce. After slices of meat have been eaten, the rest of the bird is often used to make stock for soup, which is served at the end of the meal.

The other famous dish of Beijing is the *shuanyangrou*, usually known in English as the Mongolian hotpot. More suitable for winter than summer, cooking is done at the table in boiling stock contained in a charcoal-burning metal pot with a chimney. The diners themselves plunge finely sliced mutton into the stock, then vegetables, beancurd, and vermicelli.

Beijing has a long-established tradition of possessing excellent restaurants which offer the best of China's many regional cuisines. This reputation is still well justified, and first-class restaurants serve food from Sichuan, Shanxi, Shandong, Qinghai, Canton and Shanghai.

Most foreigners travelling in groups, drink Chinese beer or sweet Chinese-produced soft drinks. Chinese wines are mostly quite sweet, although dry grape wines, both red and white, are increasingly available in places where foreigners eat. There are some excellent rice wines, such as Shaoxing. The highly potent Chinese spirit *maotai*, made from sorghum, is good for any flagging social occasion and is a great stimulus to speechmaking, but it is an acquired taste. Although imported alcohol is not usually served in restaurants, it is possible to buy quite a wide range of imported wines and spirits, as well as Coca-Cola and other foreign-brand soft drinks, in hotel shops. In recent years, a wide range of fruit and cola-type drinks has come on the market, as well as several brands of Chinese mineral water. Some are excellent.

Most of the restaurants listed below are used to preparing set banquets for visitors, served in private rooms. But while a private dining room may be preferable for a special occasion or for large groups, the adventurous diner going out alone, or in a small group, should not be deterred from asking to eat in the same part of the restaurant as the local Chinese.

The quantity of food served at a banquet can sometimes be overwhelming—there may be as many as 15 courses. One way to avoid this is, when booking the meal, to stipulate only five or six courses and a low price per head. Banquet prices in Beijing generally range from Rmb50–250 a head, depending on the restaurant. Restaurants tend to close very early in Beijing. It is almost always necessary to book in advance. A CITS guide or hotel staff can help you to do this. For more adventurous dining one can stroll the streets of Donghuamen and Dengshikou at the intersection of Wangfujing and Jinyu Hutong where each evening private vendors set up stalls and offer a wide range of specialities from their various provinces. One can make an evening of sampling regional dishes and browsing through the nightmarket which takes over the streets.

Another excellent outdoor snacks market with a fine view of the Rear Lakes is the Lotus Blossom Market at Shichahai, which begins across the street from the north entrance to Beihai Park and extends along the shore of the lake for several hundred metres. It is open for lunch and dinner, and features a variety of Beijing and other regional snacks: dumplings, steamed buns, pancakes, shashlik, almond pudding, stewed lungs etc.

Another novel dining experience can be had at one of the many restaurants in Beijing's **underground city**. In the late 60s, a huge underground network of tunnels and shelters was built as protection from nuclear attack. Now these shelters have been transformed into shops, restaurants and hotels. One entrance at 192 Xidan Jie, just north of Chang'an Jie leads to a small section of the underground city where several small restaurants are located, the best known of which is the Dongtian (Cave Heaven) restaurant.

In recent years, dozens of privately or cooperatively run restaurants have opened in every corner of the city. Some occupy old residences, others are carved out of unused factory space, but most of them provide excellent food for surprisingly low prices. Four major areas to look for these restaurants are Qianmen and Dazhalan (Dashalar); the block behind the Beijing Hotel; and in the Dongdan and Dongsi shopping areas. Perhaps the best way to judge a restaurant is whether or not it is crowded.

Virtually all international-standard hotels have top-quality Chinese restaurants. Although perhaps not as exciting as dining out in a local restaurant, these hotels offer some of the best Chinese food in the city, with polished service to match. For Cantonese food (prepared under the professional eye of Hong Kong chefs), you could try the **Four Seasons** at the Jianguo (tel. 5002233) which serves a particularly good *dim sum* (11.30 am–2 pm); the Jinglun's **Tao Li**, which specializes in both Cantonese and Chaozhou dishes (tel. 5002266), the **Fan** at the Great Wall Sheraton (tel. 5005566), the **Spring Garden** at the Holiday Inn Lido (tel. 5006688), and the refined **Shang Palace** at the Shangri-La (tel. 8312211). The Great Wall Sheraton's **Yuan Tai** offers classic Sichuan delicacies, together with a panoramic view from the 22nd floor of the hotel.

Recent additions to the roster of luxurious hotel restaurants are **Fortune Garden** Cantonese restaurant and the **Palace Restaurant** Sichuan restaurant at the Palace Hotel (tel. 5128899), the **Summer Palace** restaurant at the **China World Hotel** (tel. 5052266).

For Shanghai food, try the **Shanghai Restaurant** in the Kunlun Hotel (tel. 5003388).

Beijing and Shandong

Beijing Duck Restaurants (Beijing Kaoya Dian) 北京烤鸭店

A Beijing duck banquet may consist of far more than just the serving of the crisp skin and meat of the tender bird, accompanied by pancakes, sesame buns, scallions and thick brown fermented sauce. Cold duck dishes—which may include meat in aspic, shredded webs, and sliced liver—are usually served first, followed by fried duck heart, liver and gizzard, and the delicious duck soup which comes at the very end of the meal.

Most visitors to Beijing want to try the famous duck dinner and, as a result, the branches of the official Beijing Duck Restaurant tend to turn out rather routine meals. Opinions vary on the best place to go to sample Beijing duck, but many would favour the small restaurant off Wangfujing, known locally as the 'Sick Duck' because of its proximity to the Capital Hospital. Other branches are the 'Small Duck', the 'Big Duck' and the 'Super Duck' (a four-storey modern building that can seat about 2,000 people at one time).

Clay Saucepan (Shaguoju) 沙锅居 西四南大街60号
60 Xisi Nan Dajie. Tel. 661126, 661123

This is the oldest restaurant in Beijing, claiming a history which goes back some 300 years. Perhaps the best known all-pork restaurant in Asia, it is said to have originated as a shop selling off pigs that the emperor had sacrificed for a good harvest. An all-pork banquet can be ordered in advance, or it is possible to try just a few of the famous dishes, such as deep fried pork liver or fried pork ribs, along with various soups and vegetables dishes.

Confucius Restaurant 孔膳堂饭店 玻璃厂西街 3 号
3 Liulichang Xi Jie. Tel. 330689

Crowded restaurant featuring the cuisine of Confucius' native place and banquets as prepared in the hereditary mansion of the Kong family (Confucius was surnamed Kong). Located in Liulichang across the street from the China Book Store. Try the deep fried scorpion!

Donglaishun 东来顺饭店 东华门16号
16 Donghuamen, at the north entrance of Dongfeng Market. Tel. 550069

This is an excellent place to try Mongolian hotpot in unpretentious surroundings with pleasant service. Highly popular with the people of Beijing, this restaurant is always busy. The lamb shashlik—chunks of lamb rolled in sesame seed and barbecued—is specially good, and for the more adventurous there are other Mongolian specialities to try such as braised camel's hump or camel tendons.

Duyichu 都一处烧卖馆 前门大街36号
36 Qianmen Dajie. Tel. 5112094

Centuries old institution that serves famous *shaomai* steamed dumpling and Shandong cuisine.

'Sick Duck' (Wangfujing Kaoya Dian) 王府井烤鸭店　师府园13号
13 Shuaifuyuan. Tel. 553310

'Small Duck' (Pianyifang Kaoya Dian) 便宜坊烤鸭店　崇文门外大街2号
2 Chongwenmenwai Dajie. Tel. 755007, 750505

'Big Duck' (Qianmen Kaoya Dian) 前门烤鸭店　前门大街24号
32 Qianmen Dajie. Tel. 5112418

'Super Duck' (Heping Kaoya Dian) 和平烤鸭店　宣武门大街
Xuanwumen Dajie. Tel. 338031

Fangshan 仿膳饭店　北海公园
Beihai Park. Tel. 4011879, 442573

This prestigious restaurant opened in Beihai Park in 1925, uses recipes from the
19th-century imperial Court. Banquets are highly elaborate and expensive—a
meal including delicacies such as sharksfin and bird's nest soup might cost over
Rmb200 a head. When the restaurant first opened it was considered to be the
best in Beijing, although today some westerners find the food over-rich and
indigestible. But with a magnificent setting on an island in the centre of the
beautiful lake in Beihai Park, this must surely rank as one of the most splendid
restaurants in China.

Kangle 康乐餐馆　安定门内大街259号
259 Andingmennei Dajie. Tel. 443884

Although the food at the Kangle is predominantly northern, the restaurant is
famous for its dishes from Yunnan, the province in the far southwest of China.
The best-known dish here is called 'crossing the bridge noodles'—noodles
cooked in chicken stock. There are several versions of how the dish acquired its
intriguing name. One claims that noodles which were destined for the emperor's
table were dropped into a pot of boiling water at the bridge which led into the
Imperial Palace. By the time the pot had reached the table, the noodles were
exactly ready to be served up. Try some of the excellent soups that are served
here, as well as the delicious Yunnan chicken, steamed in oil and delicately
flavoured with herbs.

Kaorouji 北京烤肉店　什刹前海东沿14号
14 Shishaqianhai Dong Yan. Tel. 4012170

This small and sometimes expensive restaurant specializing in Mongolian barbecued lamb is sought out by discriminating visitors. Situated just north of Beihai Park in the Rear Lakes district, the restaurant has a balcony which looks out over an interesting neighbourhood.

Li Jia Cai (Li Family Restaurant) 李家菜餐厅 德内大街杨坊胡同11号
11 Yangfang Hutong, Denei Dajie. Tel. 6011915

Small privately run restaurant open for dinner only. Dishes from the Qing Court—Reservations recommended.

Pavilion for Listening to the Orioles (Tingliguan) 听鹂馆 颐和园
Yiheyuan. Tel 2581608, 2581955, 2582504

In attractive rooms round a courtyard in the heart of the Summer Palace, this lunch restaurant is very popular with western visitors. The food is an eclectic mixture of different Chinese styles, all of the dishes appealing to foreigners. Try the deep fried steamed bread and the fresh fish from the Summer Palace's Kunming Lake.

Ritan Park Restaurant 日坛公园饭店 日坛公园
Ritan Park. Tel. 5004984, 5005837

This little restaurant in the southwest corner of the Temple of the Sun Park is located in a delightful courtyard beside a small pond complete with arching bridges and pavilions. It is possible to eat outside when the weather permits. It is particularly popular for its very good *jiaozi*—steamed dumplings.

Tan Family Cuisine (Tan jia cai) 谭家菜餐厅 北京饭店东长安街33号
Beijing Hotel. 33 Dong Chang'an Jie. Tel. 5137766

A sub-school of Beijing cooking founded in the 19th century that features seafood. It is named after a cantonese official who lived in Beijing and hired the best chefs in the capital to cook for them. The entire repertoire consists of approximately 100 dishes developed in their kitchens.

Cantonese

Beijing Orient Restaurant 北京东方明珠酒家 前门西大街正阳市场 4 号楼
Zhengyang Market, Qianmenxi Dajie. Tel. 3016688

One of the best Cantonese restaurants in the city, the Beijing Orient is pure Hong Kong.

Chaozhoufang Restaurant 潮州房饭店 西直门街135号
135 Xizhimen Jie. Tel. 8021450

Chaozhou is in Guangdong Province yet its cuisine is quite distinct from typical Cantonese-style cooking, using less sugar and a unique blend of spices and aromatics. The origin of Chaozhou cooking is not certain but one story claims that the style evolved after a minister of the Ming court was banished to this region for poor conduct. The minister, unsatisfied with the local culinary fare, set about instructing cooks on how to enhance certain flavours, and he passed his time experimenting with many local ingredients. The result was a dramatically new cuisine.

Dasanyuan 大三院 京山西街50号
50 Jingshan Xi Jie. Tel. 4013920

Outside the joint-venture hotels, this is one of the few authentic Cantonese restaurants in Beijing and is quite pricey. Meat and vegetables are brought in daily from Guangdong Province to supply the restaurant with its many specialities, which include roast suckling pig, dog meat, seafood, chicken cooked in tea, turtle meat and special seasonal dishes such as 'battle between the dragon and the tiger'—cat meat with three kinds of snake—and crab and giant salamander.

Dynasty Restaurant　王朝餐厅　京广中心
4/F, Jing Guang Centre, Hu Jia Lou, Chaoyang District. Tel. 5108888, extn. 2599

Fortune Garden　王府饭店　王府井
Palace Hotel, Wangfujing. Tel. 5128899, extn. 7405

Maintains the high standards associated with the Peninsula Hotel in Hong Kong.

Renren Restaurant　人人大酒楼　前门东大街18号
18 Qianmen Dong Dajie. Tel. 5112978

This large four-storey, joint-venture restaurant features Cantonese food and does lively business. With each successive floor, the dishes become increasingly exotic and expensive. The restaurant's specialities include many standard Cantonese dishes such as suckling pig braised in barbeque sauce, shark's fin and dog. Although the decor is a bit heavily ornate with large red columns and glass-fringed light fixtures, the atmosphere is casual and friendly.

Moslem

Hongbinlou　鸿宾楼　西长安街82号
82 Xi Chang'an Jie. Tel. 656404, 657941, 655691

This long-established Moslem restaurant, serving no pork, has been open for nearly a century, and continues to specialize in some of Beijing's favourite dishes—Beijing duck, Mongolian hotpot, and pieces of lamb barbecued on skewers—but its wide menu includes many other famous dishes well worth trying, such as sliced sautéed eel, and chicken breasts in red sauce.

Huimin Kaorouwan　回民烤肉丸　宣武门西单南102号
102 Xidan Nan, Xuanwumen. Tel. 330700

Serving a variety of Moslem-style dishes, this restaurant's speciality is barbecued mutton. This dish is particularly enjoyable during the winter, when you may stand around special barbecue stoves and cook the thin strips of mutton yourself, adding noodles, onions and eggs as you like.

Jenghiz Khan Restaurant　成吉思汗酒家　亮马桥安家楼
Anjialou, Liangmaqiao Lu. Tel. 471614

On His Baldness

At dawn I sighed to see my hairs fall;
At dusk I sighed to see my hairs fall.
For I dreaded the time when the last lock should go . . .
They are all gone and I do not mind at all!
I have done with that cumbrous washing and getting dry;
My tiresome comb for ever is laid aside.
Best of all, when the weather is hot and wet,
To have no top-knot weighing down on one's head!
I put aside my messy cloth wrap;
I have got rid of my dusty tasselled fringe.
In a silver jar I have stored a cold stream,
On my bald pate I trickle a ladle full.
Like one baptized with the Water of Buddha's Law,
I sit and receive this cool, cleansing joy.
Now I know why the priest who seeks Repose
Frees his heart by first shaving his head.

'Lazy Man's Song'

I could have a job, but am too lazy to choose it;
I have got land, but am too lazy to farm it.
My house leaks; I am too lazy to mend it.
My clothes are torn; I am too lazy to darn them.
I have got wine, but I am too lazy to drink;
So it's just the same as if my cup were empty.
I have got a lute, but am too lazy to play;
So it's just the same as if it had no strings.
My family tells me there is no more steamed rice;
I want to cook, but am too lazy to grind.
My friends and relatives write me long letters;
I should like to read them, but they're such a bother to open.
I have always been told that Hsi Shu-yeh
Passed his whole life in absolute idleness.
But he played his lute and sometimes worked at his forge;
So even he *was not so lazy as I.*

Po Chü-I, 772–846 A D

The enterprising owner of a small inn for Mongolian travellers coming to Beijing had the bright idea of setting up this authentic Mongolian restaurant in two yurts; one has low Mongolian-style seating and the other regular seating. The traditional menu includes leg of lamb, kebabs, even whole lamb, as well as Mongolian hotpot and boiled duck—all served by staff in Mongolian dress. A meal costs between Rmb30–80 a head. Set out on a dusty road, northeast from the Great Wall Sheraton, this is definitely a restaurant for adventurous eaters. It has quickly become a favourite with the expatriate community and reservations are essential.

Qinghai

Qinghai Restaurant 青海餐厅 东四北大街555号
555 Dongsi Bei Dajie. Tel. 442947

The speciality of this restaurant is 'chicken with caterpillars'—chicken stuffed with a fungus found in the distant western Chinese province of Qinghai which is called 'winter worm, summer grass'—and looks exactly like a small caterpillar. Dog meat and shashlik are also served here.

Shandong

Cuihualou 萃华楼 王府井60号
50 Wangfujing. Tel. 554581

A popular and long established restaurant serving Shandong-style food. Among its specialities is 'peak flower rice'—crispy-rice over which is poured, in front of you at the table, a sweet and sour prawn sauce, so that it hisses and pops and must be eaten quickly before the rice turns soggy.

Garden of the Horn of Plenty (Fengzeyuan) 丰泽园 珠市口西大街83号
Two locations: Xinfu sancun, Dongzhimenwai. Tel. 4217508
Liujiayao, Yongdingmenwai. Tel. 7211331

One of Beijing's most famous eating houses, the Fengzeyuan is celebrated for its Shandong food. The cuisine of this coastal province south of Beijing includes some excellent fish dishes. Particularly well known here are the sea cucumber, soup with cuttle-fish eggs, and braised fish with a rich brown sauce. The restaurant enjoys a high reputation, and banquets here are invariably good.

Hongxinglou 鸿星楼　北纬路1号
1 Beiwei Lu. Tel. 332015, 334158

This restaurant serves typical North China cuisine and, besides a repertoire of
200 Shandong provincial dishes, also boasts of 20 different kinds of *jiaozi*—
steamed dumpling with tasty fillings; try their *guo tie*—steamed dumplings
which have been lightly fried.

Tongheju 同和居／西四南大街3号
3 Xisi Nan Dajie. Tel. 660925

A Shandong-style restaurant with private dining rooms off a small courtyard in
the northwestern part of the city. Seafood specialities include sea cucumber,
'squirrel fish' in sweet sauce, jumbo prawns in various styles, and crab and eel
in season. Steamed white bread rolls are popular here and their dessert is famous
throughout Beijing—'three no sticks'—an elusively flavoured but delicious
custard, made from egg yolks and cornflour with an extraordinary texture—
whence its name comes—'won't stick to your plate, won't stick to your chopsticks and won't stick to your palate'.

Shanghai

Laozhengxing 老正兴饭庄　前门大街46号
46 Qianmen Dajie. Tel. 5112145

Named after a famous restaurant in Shanghai, Laozhengxing features authentic
Shanghai cuisine with an emphasis on seafood.

Shanxi

Jinyang 晋阳饭店　珠市口西大街241号
241 Zhushikou Xi Dajie. Tel. 331669

This interesting restaurant in the southern section of the city is in the house
formerly used by Mei Lanfang (1894–1961), the most famous of all Beijing
opera singers, for his National Theatre Study Group. The finest rooms in the
house now serve as impressive dining rooms. The kitchens specialize in the
cuisine of Shanxi. This is the perfect setting to try the delicious crisp duck of the
province—to some western palates preferable to the rich Beijing duck.

Sichuan

Dou Hua Village   豆昆村   日坛公园（西南方入口）
Ritan Park (southwest entrance). Tel. 5005939

Popular outdoor/indoor restaurant in the embassy district. Make a meal of the varied snack menu. Pleasant garden-like atmosphere.

Rong Yuan   荣苑   北京贵宾楼饭店东长安街33号
Grand Hotel, 33 Dong Chang'an Jie. Tel. 5137788

Teahouse style restaurant in a new luxury hotel.

Sichuan   四川饭店   绒线胡同51号
51 Rongxian Hutong. Tel. 656348

This elegant restaurant in attractive traditional old buildings with dining rooms arranged round a series of courtyards is the most famous Sichuan restaurant in China, specializing in the hot spicy cuisine of the large southwestern province. Any of the many specialities here is worth trying. The smoke duck, spiced beancurd, and braised egg-plant have been specially recommended. Some of the finer dishes are not spicy.

Sichuan Dou Hua Restaurant   四川豆花饭庄   广渠门外
Guangumenwai. Tel. 7712672

This new three-storey restaurant has a rather original character; in the upstairs dining rooms, women in traditional Sichuan costumes serve you while men in black tunics steadily refill your teacup. All of this takes place in charmingly decorated private dining rooms. The menu offers all of Sichuan's best known dishes such as hot peanut chicken, spicy doufu, and noodles in *dandan* sauce. For the unacquainted, this restaurant is a wonderful introduction to authentic Sichuan cooking.

Suzhou

Songhelou   松鹤楼菜馆   台基厂大街10号
10 Taijichang Jie. Tel. 545223

The original Songhelou was in Suzhou, where it specialized in the delicate, tender, slightly sweet cuisine of the city, which was particularly favoured by Emperor Qianlong. Recommended in the Beijing restaurant are dishes typical of the Suzhou area—squirrel-shaped mandarin fish, beggar's chicken, turtle with white sauce, Tai Lake greens soup, and winter mushrooms with bamboo shoots. Songhelou's banquet rooms are modelled on the original Suzhou restaurant.

Vegetarian

Beijing Vegetarian Restaurant 北京素香斋 宣武门内大街74号
74 Xuanwumennei Dajie. Tel. 654296

The Chinese are masters at the art of vegetarian cooking, and are capable of producing an astonishing variety of dishes from beancurd and wheat gluten, which forms the basis of their vegetarian food. These restaurants can provide a well-balanced banquet of as many as 15 dishes that seem like pork, duck or fish, together with fresh vegetables, many different kinds of mushrooms and seaweed, steamed dumplings and noodles.

Gongdelin 功德林素菜馆 前门南大街158号
158 Qianmennan Dajie. Tel. 750867

The original Gongdelin is in Shanghai. Atmosphere here is somewhat more refined than at the Beijing Vegetarian Restaurant but menu is similar.

Indian

Shamiana Indian Restaurant 京都假日饭店印度菜餐厅
Holiday Inn Downtown, 98 Beilishi Lu, Western district. Tel. 8322288
北京金都假日饭店　西城区北礼士路98号
The first 'serious' Indian restaurant in Beijing opened to a warm reception.

Japanese

Beijing now has at least a dozen high-quality Japanese restaurants, serving mostly the large Japanese expatriate community in Beijing as well as the many Japanese tour groups that visit the city. Interestingly, Japanese food in Beijing is reputedly the least expensive high quality Japanese food in the world.

Baiyun Restaurant 白云日本餐厅 友好宾馆后圆恩寺7号
Youhao Guesthouse, 7 Houyuanensi, Jiaodaokou. Tel. 441036

This intimate restaurant is down a secluded *hutong,* and is part of the Youhao Guesthouse complex where Chiang Kai-Shek used to live when he visited Beijing. The quiet surroundings create a tranquil atmosphere that is unusual in modern Beijing. The restaurant serves fresh sushi, sashimi, seafood tempura, as well as teriyaki, tempura and sukiyaki. It is open every evening 6–11 pm except Mondays.

Duoweizhai 多味斋 新源里
Xinyuanli. Tel. 484591

The chefs here are Japanese, the waiters wear traditional dress, and the extensive menu covers sushi, sashimi, teriyaki, sukiyaki, tempura, with an impressive range of appetizers and numerous kinds of sake. Traditional private rooms with floor-seating may be booked. The restaurant is rather large and animated, lacking the intimacy of traditional Japanese restaurants. It is open for lunch 11.30 am–2 pm, and stays open late by Beijing standards for dinner from 5.30 pm to midnight.

Inagiku 日本菜餐厅 王府饭店 王府井
Palace Hotel, Wangfujing. Tel. 5128899

Nakabachi 日本菜餐厅 建国饭店 建国门外大街
Jianguo Hotel, Jianguomenwai Dajie. Tel. 5002233, extn. 2197

One of the first Japanese restaurants in the city, it continues to maintain high standards.

Sakura 樱花园 长富宫饭店 建国门外大街
Chang Fu Gong New Otani Hotel, Jianguomenwai Dajie. Tel. 5125555 extn. 1226

Korean

Warming diplomatic relations and increased trade between China and South Korea has given rise to a number of restaurants specializing in Korean barbecue, cold noodles and dog meat.

Bobea Wan 北京国际饭店朝鲜菜餐厅 北京国际饭店 建国门内大街 9 号
Beijing International Hotel, 9 Jianguomenwai Dajie. Tel. 5129844

Go Nin Byakushou 北京饭店朝鲜菜餐厅 北京饭店 东长安街
Beijing Hotel, Dongchang'an Jie. Tel. 5137766

Mu Dan Feng 牡丹峰餐厅 南河沿路华龙街商业中心
Hualong Jie Food Street, Nanheyan Lu. Tel. 5125133

Thai

Borom Piman   泰国菜餐厅   北京丽都假日饭店   首都机场路将台路
Holiday Inn Lido, Jichang Lu. Tel. 5006688

Li Yuan Restaurant   利苑饭店   西皇城根街 8 号
8 Xihuang Chenggen. Tel. 6015234

Beijing's first Thai restaurant. The manager and chefs are all originally from
Thailand. The restaurant's celebrated dish in *Tomyan Koong*, a prawn soup
spiced with lime juice, hot chili and coriander.

Western

Beijing's foreign-managed hotels, with European chefs heading up the kitchen
staff, have greatly improved the standard of western cooking in the capital. Ten
years ago, it was almost impossible to find acceptable—sometimes even recognizable—western food. Although none of Beijing's western restaurants can
match Hong Kong's best, the foreign-managed hotels have good European
restaurants, with pleasant service, and a palatable, although not extensive wine
list. (Wine prices are very high, largely because of hefty import duties.) For
many foreign visitors to China, dining in a soft-lit leisurely atmosphere makes a
welcome change from the austere and hurried mood of many Chinese restaurants. Because so many of the ingredients still have to be imported, as well as
the staff to prepare them, you should expect to pay a lot for a European meal.

The Shangri-La's **La Brasserie** is probably the finest western restaurant in
Beijing. At the Great Wall Sheraton is the elegant **La France**, and at the Holiday Inn Lido, the **Marco**, which also has a good lunchtime buffet. Many regular
visitors to Beijing favour **Justine's** in the Jianguo, where you may dine by
candlelight in the evenings. A pleasant alternative is **Dynasty**, the European
restaurant in the next-door Jinglun. The **Roma** Italian restaurant in the Palace
Hotel enjoys a high reputation. Make reservations early for all these. The joint-
venture hotels make special efforts for Sunday lunches or brunches, and the
Holiday Inn's Friday evening curry buffet on the **Patio** has become something
of an institution. Food promotions are usually advertised in *China Daily*.

German specialities are served at **Baurenstube** at the **Holiday Inn Lido**, and
at **Bavaria Bierstube**, a casual cafe-bar in the basement of the **Palace Hotel**.

Italian food is represented by four hotel venues: **Peppino's** in the **Shangri-
la**, **Pinochio** in the **Holiday Inn Lido**, the much touted **Roma** in the **Palace
Hotel**, and **Toula** in the **Beijing International Hotel**.

American fare is available at **Prime Cut** at the **China World Hotel** and at the American-style bar, **Pete's Place**, at the **Beijing Exhibition Centre Hotel** near the Beijing Zoo.

The **Landmark Hotel** next to the Great Wall Sheraton has an attractive **Food Court** featuring a variety of cuisines. International-style coffee shops can be found in every major joint venture hotel. The Jianguo is a favourite for American-style hamburgers. Of the Chinese-run hotels, the best European food is to be had at the **Minzu**, where the revamped ground-floor restaurant has some specialities that match their much more expensive foreign-run counterparts.

Moscow (Exhibition Centre) Restaurant (Beijing Zhanlanguan Fandian)
Xizhimenwai Dajie. Tel. 893713
莫斯科餐厅　西外大街北京展览馆
Opened in 1954, this is an interesting legacy of the Russian presence in Beijing. With its immense dining room and high ceilings, the restaurant's severe decor is evocative of the Russian architecture of the 50s. And the wide European menu still retains a strong Slavic flavour. Caviar (a Chinese variety but quite palatable), bortsch, and excellent chicken Kiev served in generous portions, are all worth trying.

Kentucky Fried Chicken　肯德基家乡鸡　天安门正阳市场
1 Tiananmen Zhengyangzshichang. Tel. 3014131. Other outlets can be found at: the Dongsi intersection. Tel. 557087; and Hualongjie Food Street. Tel. 5124130

The opening of this well-known US fast food chain was the first of its kind in China. Situated at the southwest corner of Tiananmen Square, diners are afforded a rare view of the Mao Mausoleum with the Gate of Heavenly Peace in the distance. Prices are reasonable, the staff are friendly and efficient, and it is in a prime location making this a popular place among local Chinese and foreign residents.

Maxim de Pékin 马克西姆餐厅 前门东大街 2 号
2 Qianmen Dong Dajie. Tel. 5122110 (reservations), 5121992 (bar)

Owned by Pierre Cardin, this restaurant astonished the city when it first opened in 1983, not just because of its decor, but also on account of the apparently genuine French cuisine, the polished service, and the very high prices. Now, with the appearance of several other quality European restaurants in new hotels, Maxim's is less of a curiosity. Prices have levelled out, and the restaurant is well patronized by diplomats, expatriates and business visitors who like to entertain high-ranking officials there. The menu reads as a Maxim's menu should—Fois Gras de Canard fait Maison, Crépes Fourrées Suzette, Mousse Glacée Flambôise, Iced Soufflé Grand Marnier, Escargots Fricassée. The wine list is good by Beijing standards. After 9 pm, you may go just for drinks at the bar, where there is a small dancefloor. Downstairs is an economical version of Maxim's cutely called **Minim**'s featuring full course French meals and a more modest menu than its upstairs neighbour.

Pizza Hut 必胜客比萨饼屋 东直门外大街
Dongzhimenwai Dajie. Tel. 4662667

Useful Addresses

Embassies

Albania
28 Guanghua Lu, Jianguomenwai.
Tel. 511120
亚尔巴尼亚　建国门外光华路28号

Argentina
11 Sanlitun Dongwu Jie. Tel. 5322090
阿根廷　三里屯东五街11号

Australia
15 Dongzhimenwai Dajie, Sanlitun.
Tel. 5322331–7
澳大利亚　三里屯东直门外大街15号

Austria
5 Xiushui Nan Jie, Jianguomenwai.
Tel. 5322061–3
奥地利　建国门外秀水南街5号

Bangladesh
42 Guanghua Lu, Jianguomenwai.
Tel. 5322521
孟加拉国　建国门外光华路42号

Belgium
6 Sanlitun Lu. Tel. 5321736–8
比利时　三里屯6号

Brazil
27 Guanghua Lu, Jianguomenwai.
Tel. 5322881, 5323883
巴西　建国门外光华路27号

Burma
6 Dongzhimenwai Dajie, Sanlitun.
Tel. 5321425
缅甸　三里屯东直门外大街6号

Canada
10 Sanlitun Lu. Tel. 5323536
加拿大　三里屯10号

Czechoslovakia
Ritan Lu, Jianguomenwai. Tel. 5321530–1
捷克斯拉夫　建国门外日坛路

Denmark
1 Sanlitun Dongwu Jie. Tel. 5322431
丹麦　三里屯东五街1号

Finland
30 Guanghua Lu, Jianguomenwai.
Tel. 5321817, 5321806
芬兰　建国门外光华路30号

France
3 Sanlitun Dongsan Jie. Tel. 5321331
法国　三里屯东三街3号

Germany, Federal Republic of
5 Dongzhimenwai Dajie, Sanlitun.
Tel. 5322161
西德国　三里屯东直门外大街5号

Ghana
8 Sanlitun Lu. Tel. 5321319
加纳　三里屯8号

India
1 Ritan Dong Lu, Jianguomenwai.
Tel. 5321908, 5321856
印度　建国门外日坛东路1号

Italy
2 Sanlitun Donger Jie. Tel. 5322131
意大利　三里屯东二街2号

Japan
7 Ritan Lu, Jianguomenwai. Tel. 5322361
日本　建国门外日坛路7号

Jordan
54 Sanlitun Dongliu Jie. Tel. 5323906
约旦　三里屯东六街54号

Kampuchea
9 Dongzhimenwai Dajie. Tel. 5321889
柬埔寨　东直门外大街

Kenya
4 Sanlitun Xiliu Jie. Tel. 5323381
肯尼亚　三里屯西六街

Kuwait
23 Guanghua Lu, Jianguomenwai.
Tel. 5322182
科威特　建国门外光华路23号

Laos
11 Sanlitun Dongsi Jie. Tel. 5321224
老挝　三里屯东四街11号

Malaysia
13 Dongzhimenwai Dajie, Sanlitun.
Tel. 5322531
马来西亚　三里屯东直门外大街13号

Nepal
1 Sanlitun Xiliu Jie. Tel. 5321795
尼泊尔　三里屯西六街1号

New Zealand
1 Ritan Donger Jie, Jianguomenwai.
Tel. 5322731–4
新西兰　建国门外日坛东二街1号

Nigeria
2 Dongwu Jie, Sanlitun Bei. Tel. 5323631
尼日利亚　三里屯东五街2号

Norway
1 Sanlitun Dongyi Jie. Tel. 5322261–2
挪威　三里屯东一街1号

Pakistan
1 Dongzhimenwai Dajie, Sanlitun.
Tel. 5322504
巴基斯坦　三里屯东直门外大街1号

Philippines
23 Xiushui Bei Jie, Jianguomenwai.
Tel. 5322794
菲律宾　建国门外秀水北街23号

Poland
1 Ritan Lu, Jianguomenwai.
Tel. 5321235
波兰　建国门外日坛路1号

Sierra Leone
7 Dongzhimenwai Dajie, Sanlitun.
Tel. 5321446
塞拉利昂　三里屯东直门外大街7号

Singapore
4 Liangmahe Nan Lu, Sanlitun.
Tel. 5323926
新加坡　三里屯亮马河南路4号

Spain
9 Sanlitun Lu. Tel. 5323629, 5321986
西班牙　三里屯路9号

Sri Lanka
3 Jianhua Lu, Jianguomenwai. Tel.
5321861–2
斯里兰卡　建国门外建华路3号

Sweden
3 Dongzhimenwai Dajie, Sanlitun.
Tel. 5323331
瑞典　三里屯东直门外大街3号

Switzerland
3 Sanlitun Dongwu Jie. Tel. 5322736–8
瑞士　三里屯东五街3号

Tanzania
53 Sanlitun, Dongliu Jie. Tel. 5321408
坦桑尼亚　三里屯东六街53号

Thailand
40 Guanghua Lu, Jianguomenwai.
Tel. 5321903
泰国　建国门外光华路40号

Chronology of Periods in Chinese History

Paleolithic	c.600,000–7000 BC
Neolithic	c. 7000–1600 BC
Shang	c.1600–1027 BC
Western Zhou	1027–771 BC
Eastern Zhou	770–256 BC
Spring and Autumn Annals	770–476 BC
Warring States	475–221 BC
Qin	221–207 BC
Western (Former) Han	206 BC–AD 8
Xin	9–24
Eastern (Later) Han	25–220
Three Kingdoms	220–265
Western Jin	265–316
Northern and Southern Dynasties	317–581
Sixteen Kingdoms	317–439
Former Zhao	304–329
Former Qin	351–383
Later Qin	384–417
Northern Wei	386–534
Western Wei	535–556
Northern Zhou	557–581
Sui	581–618
Tang	618–907
Five Dynasties	907–960
Northern Song	960–1127
Southern Song	1127–1279
Jin (Jurchen)	1115–1234
Yuan (Mongol)	1279–1368
Ming	1368–1644
Qing (Manchu)	1644–1911
Republic of China	1911–1949
People's Republic of China	1949–

Uganda
5 Sanlitun Dong Jie. Tel. 5321708
乌干达　三里屯东街5号

United Kingdom
11 Guanghua Lu. Jianguomenwai.
Tel. 5321961–5
英国　建国门外光华路11号

USA
(Consular section)
2 Ziushui Dong Jie. Jianguomenwai.
Tel. 5323431
美国　建国门外秀水东街2号

USSR
4 Dongzhimen Beizhong Jie. Tel. 5322051,
5321381
苏联　东直门北中街4号

Venezuela
14 Sanlitun Lu. Tel. 5321295
委内瑞拉　三里屯路14号

Vietnam
32 Guanghua Lu, Jianguomenwai.
Tel. 5321155, 5321125
越南　建国门外光华路32号

Yugoslavia
56 Sanlitun Dongliu Jie. Tel. 5321562
南斯拉夫　三里屯东六街56号

Zambia
5 Sanlitun Dongsi Jie. Tel. 5321554
赞比亚　三里屯东四街

Airlines

Aeroflot Soviet Airlines
5–53 Jianguomenwai. Tel. 5323581
苏联航空公司　建国门外5-53号

Air China
Airport Office. Tel. 5138833, 558341.
Tlx. 210322
Beijing Booking Office, 117 Dongsi Xi
Dajie.
Tel. 4013331, 4014441, 4012221
Freight. Tel. 473167
中国国际航空公司　首都飞机场/东四西
大街117号
Air China (Beijing Hotel)
Chang'an Dajie. Tel. 5137317
中国民航(北京饭店)　长安大街

Air China (Great Wall Sheraton)
Donghuan Bei Lu. Tel. 5002272
中国民航(长城饭店)　东环北路

Alitalia
Jianguo Hotel. Tel. 5002233 extn. 139–140
意大利空公司　建国门外150号

All Nippon Airways
2073/5 Beijing Hotel
Tel. 5125551
全日空航空公司　北京饭店20735房

British Airways
Rm 210, SCITE Tower,
22 Jianguomenwai.
Tel. 5124070
英国航空公司　建国门外 22 号
賽特大厦 210 室

Canadian Airlines International
Rm 135, Jianguo Hotel, Jianguomenwai.
Tel. 5001956, 5002233 extn. 135
加拿大国际航空公司　建国门外建国饭店134房

Dragonair
L107, 1/fl, China World Trade Centre
1 Jianguomenwai Dajie. Tel. 5054343
港龙航空公司　建国门外大街 1 号中国国际
贸易中心国贸大厦 1 楼 L107室。

Ethiopian Airlines
12–32 Jianguomenwai. Tel. 5323285
埃塞俄比亚航空公司　建国门外12-32号

Finnair
CITIC Building, Jianguomenwai.
Tel. 512780
芬兰航空公司　建国门外国际大厦1-2号

Interfug
Rm 107, Holiday Inn Lido Hotel.
Tel. 5006618, 5006676
民主德国民航公司　丽都假日饭店1406房

Iran Air
Holiday Inn Lido Hote Jiangumenwai,
Tel. 5006676, 5006678
伊朗航空公司　丽都假日饭店

Iraqi Airways
Building 7–1–54
Diplomate Apartments, Jianguomenwai.
Tel.5321379
伊拉克航空公司　建国门外

Japan Airlines
Jinglun Hotel, Jianguomenwai.
Tel. 5002221
日本航空公司　建国门外京伦饭店

JAT Ygoslav Airlines
Kunlun Hotel. Tel. 5003388 extn. 426–7
南斯拉夫航空公司　昆仑饭店

Chosonminhang (North Korea)
Ritan Bei Lu, Jianguomenwai.
Tel. 5323981
朝鲜民用航空局　建国门外日坛北路

LOT Polish Airlines
Jianguo Hotel, Jianguomenwai.
Tel. 556720 extn. 139
波兰航空公司　建国门外建国饭店

Lufthansa
2nd Floor, SCITE Tower. Tel. 5123535,
5123636, 5123400
德国航空公司　赛特大厦2楼

Northwest Orient
Rm 103, Jianguo Hotel. Tel. 5002233
extn. 103
西北航空公司　建国门外建国饭店103房

Pakistan International Airlines
12–43 Jianguomenwai. Tel. 5323274
巴基斯坦国际航空公司　建国门外12-43号

Airport

Beijing International Airport
Switchboard. Tel. 552515, 555402, 557395
北京国际机场

Taxis

Beijing Taxi Co.
Maquan, Guangquemenwai. Tel. 594441
Bus (telephone order) 552287
Taxi (telephone order) 557661
北京出租汽车公司　广渠门外马泉

Philippine Airlines
12–53 Jianguomenwai. Tel. 5323992
菲律宾航空公司　建国门外12-53号

Qantas Airways
Beijing–Toronto Hotel,
Jianguomenwai. Tel. 5002481
澳大利亚航空公司　建国门外京伦饭店

SAS-Scandinavian Airlines System
18th Floor, SCITE Tower.
Tel. 5120575, 5122288
斯堪的纳维亚航空公司 赛特大厦18楼

Singapore Airlines
1–2 CITIC Building, Jianguomenwai
Tel. 5004138
新加坡航空公司　建国门外国际大厦1-2号

Swissair
2nd Floor, Noble Tower. Tel. 5123555–6
瑞士航空公司　卢堡大厦2楼

Tarom Romanian Air Transport
Ritan Donger Lu, Jianguomenwai.
Tel. 5323552
罗马尼亚空运公司　建国门外日坛东二路

Thai International
207–9, Noble Tower. Tel. 5128888
泰国国际航空公司　卢堡大厦207-9号

Captial Taxi Co.
10 Yuetan Bei Jie, Xzichuengqu.
Tel. 868084, 863661
(English speaking despatch). Tel. 557461
首都出租汽车公司　西城区月坛北街10号

Railway

Main Railway Station
Foreigner's Ticket Office. Tel. 5128931
Enquiries, Tel. 554866, 5576851, 5582042
Baggage
Tel. (Domestic and international arrivals
5582372, 556956, 556028

Bicycle Rental

Dongdan Bicycle Repair Service
Dongdan Bei Dajie. Tel. 552752
东单自行车修理店　建国门外22号东单
北大街

Limin Bicycle Shop
2 Chongwenmenwai Dajie
利民自行车修理站　崇文门外大街2号

Travel Agencies

Beijing Blue Sky Travel Agency
7 Yabao Road. Tel. 5126812,
tlx. 21101 LTTSA CN
北京蓝天旅行社　雅宝路7号

Beijing Tradewinds
Rm 114, 1st Floor, International Club,
Jianguomenwai. Tel. 5025997, 5025927
tlx. 210304, fax. 5004509
北京国际四季风服务有限公司
建国门外国际俱乐部二楼114室

CITS, Beijing Branch
Jinglun Hotel, Jianguomenwai.
Tel. 5002266　extn. 2041
中国国际旅行社北京分社
建国门外京伦饭店

CITS, Beijing Branch
Huadu Hotel, 8 Xinyuan Nan Lu.
Tel. 5001166 extn. 2204
中国国际旅行社北京分社
新源南路8号华都饭店

Customs
Tel. (Export) 551619 (Import) 556242,
(Foreigners's office) 5582042
北京火车站

Xizhimen Railway Station
Xizhimenwai. Tel. 8996233
西直门火车站

Jianguomenwai Bicycle Shop
Jianguomenwai (opposite Friendship store)
Tel. 592391
建国门外自行车商店　建国门外大街

Xidan Bicycle Repair Workshop
Xuanwumennei Dajie. Tel. 332472
西单自行车修理部　宣武门内大街

CITS, Beijing Branch
Great Wall Sheraton, Donghuan Bei Lu.
Tel. 513566 extn. 2269
中国国际旅行社北京分社
东环北路长城饭店

CITS Head Office
6 Dong Chang'an Jie. Tel. 5121122,
tlx. 22350
中国国际旅行社总社　东长安街6号

CTS, Head Office
8 Dongjiaomin Xiang. Tel. 5129933,
tlx. 22847
中国旅行社总办事处　东交民巷8号

CYTS (China Youth Travel Service)
23 Dongjiaomin Xiang. Tel. 5127770,
tlx. 20024
中国青年旅行社　东交民巷23号

Intourist
1 USSR Embassy, 4 Dongzhimen
Beizhong Jie.
Tel. 5321267
苏联国际旅行社　东直门北中街1号

Reliance Travel Agency
3 Zizhuyuan Lu
Tel. 8312211, tlx. 22247 BYTA CB,
fax. 8022704
信佳旅行社　紫竹园路3号

Banking Representative Offices

Bank of America
2722–3 China World Tower, CWTC
1 Jianguomenwai Dajie. Tel. 5130619
美国美洲银行　建国门外大街1号中国国际
贸易中心国际大厦2722-3室

Bank of China (Head office)
410 Fuchengmenwai Dajie.
Tel. 606688
中国银行北京总行　阜成门内大街410号

Bank of China (Beijing branch)
19 Donganmen Dajie. Tel. 5199114,
5132214
中国银行北京分行　灯市口西街19号

Bank of Tokyo
1701 China World Trade Tower CWTC,
1 Jianguomenwai Dajie.
Tel. 5053520
东京银行　建国门外大街中国国际贸易中心
国际大厦1701室

Barclay's Bank
1211 Scite Tower, 22 Jianguomenwai
Dajie. Tel. 5122288 extn. 1211
英国巴克莱银行　建国门外大街22号
赛特大厦1211室

Royal Bank of Canada
0618–20 China World Tower, CWTC
1 Jianguomenwai Dajie. Tel. 5054205
加拿大皇家银行　建国门外大街1号

Standard Chartered Bank
14/F Hongkong Macau Centre,
1 Chaoyangmen Bei Dajie.
Tel. 5011578–9
标准渣打（麦加利）银行

**The Hongkong and Shanghai Banking
Corporation**
Room 149, Jianguo Hotel.
Tel. 5001074, 5002233 extn. 145/7/9;
tlx. 22429; fax. 5001074
香港上海汇丰银行　建国饭店149房

Theatres and Cinemas

Beijing Concert Hall
Bei Xinhua Jie. Tel. 655248
北京音乐厅　北新华街

Beijing Drama Theatre
11 Hufang Lu, Xuanwuqu.
Tel. 338149, 330537
北京戏剧院　宣武区虎坊路11号

Beijing Opera Theatre
Hufangqiao. Tel. 335390
北京京剧院　虎坊桥

Capital Cinema
46 Xi Chang'an Jie. Tel. 657574
首都电影院　西长安街46号

Capital Theatre
22 Wangfujing Dajie. Tel. 550978, 557213
首都剧场　王府井大街22号

**Central Music Conservatory
Auditorium**
43 Baojia Jie, Xicheng qu. Tel. 665044
中央音乐学院礼堂

Chinese Opera Theatre
34 Baishiqiao Lu, Haidianqu.
Tel. 894703, 895144, 894612
中国京剧院　海淀区白石桥路34号

China Opera and Dance Theatre
2 Nanhua Dong Jie, Hufang Lu.
Tel. 330252
中国歌剧舞剧院　虎坊路南华东街2号

Sports Facilities

Beijing Gymnasium
4 Tiyuguan Lu, Chongwenmenwai.
Tel. 757381 extn. 502, 7016995
北京体育馆　崇文门外体育馆路4号

Beijing Workers' Gymnasium
Gongren Tiyuchang Bei Lu.
Tel. 592961
北京工人体育馆　工人体育场北路

International Club Theatre
International Club, Ritan Lu,
Jianguomenwai. Tel. 5022207
国际俱乐部剧场　建国门外日坛路国际俱乐部

**Nationalities Cultural Palace
Auditorium**
Fuxingmennei Dajie. Tel. 662530
民族文化宫礼堂　复兴门内大街

Beijing Workers' Stadium
Gongren Tiyuchang Bei Lu.
Tel. 595505
北京工人体育场　工人体育场北路

Capital Gymnasium
Baishiqiao. Tel. 8322255
首都体育馆　白石桥

Post and Telecommunications

**Beijing Main PTT (Post, Telephone and
Telecommunications) Bureau**
Dianbao Dalou, Fuxingmennei Dajie.
Tel. 664900, 664426, 666296
北京总邮电局　复兴门内大街电报大楼

Beijing Hotel PTT
(Express mail service)
Beijing Hotel, lobby concourse.
Tel. 555358
北京饭店邮电业务特快专达组
北京饭店门廊

Beijing Telecommunications Bureau
131 Xidan Dajie. Tel. 667700, 661435
北京电信局　西单

Beijing Telegraph Office
11 Xichang'an Jie. Tel. 6014834, 664900

DHL China Office
Xiao Liangmaqiao, Liangmaqiao Lu.
Tel. 481643
中国对外贸易运输公司　小亮马桥亮马桥路

DHL Sinotrans Ltd.
Huaxia Hotel, Taipingzhuang Nanli.
Tel. 4662211

Dongdan Post Office (Parcel servece)
23 Dongdan Bei Dajie.
Tel. 555043, 555265
东单邮局包裹处　东单北大街

**International Posts and
Telecommunications Services**
(Express mail service)
23 Dongdan Bei Dajie. Tel. 336621
国际邮电业务特快专达组
东单北大街23号

International Post and Telecommunications Office
Jianguomen Bei Dajie. Tel. 5128120
国际邮电信业务组　建国门北大街

Sanlitun PTT
1–3–11 Sanlitun Bei. Tel. 5321085
三里屯邮电信业务　三里屯1-3-11

Miscellaneous

Beijing Municipal Public Security Bureau (Foreigners section)
85 Beichizi Jie. Tel. 553102
北京公安局外事科　北池子街85号

Beijing (Peking) University
Yiheyuan Lu, Haidianqu.
Tel. 282471, 2561166
北京大学　海淀区颐和园路

China International Exhibition Centre
6 Beisanhuan Xi Lu, Chaoyang.
Tel. 4664433; tlx. 210214
中国国际展览馆　朝阳北三环西路6号

Capital Hospital
1 Shuaifuyuan Hutong, Wangfujing.
Tel. 5127733
首都医院　王府井师府园胡同1号

Erligou Negotiations Building
Xizhimenwai Dajie. Tel. 8317733
二里沟谈判楼　西直门外大街

International Club
Jianguomenwai. Tel. 5322144
国际俱乐部　建国门外

Sino-Japanese Friendship Hospital
Heping Jie. Tel. 4221122
中日友好医院　和平街

S.O.S. Emergency Health Service
Kunlun Hotel, Room 438.
Tel. 5003419
心急救中心　前门西街103号

Practical information, such as telephone numbers, opening hours and hotel and restaurant prices, is notoriously subject to being outdated by changes or inflation. We welcome corrections and suggestions from guidebook users; please write to The Guidebook Company, 20 Hollywood Road, Hong Kong.

A Guide to Pronouncing Chinese Names

The official system of romanization used in China, which the visitor will find on maps, road signs and city shopfronts, is known as *Pinyin*. It is now almost universally adopted by the western media.

Some visitors may initially encounter some difficulty in pronouncing romanized Chinese words. In fact many of the sounds correspond to the usual pronunciation of the letters in English. The exceptions are:

Initials

c	is like the *ts* in 'i*ts*'
q	is like the *ch* in '*ch*eese'
x	has no English equivalent, and can best be described as a hissing consonant that lies somewhere between *sh* and *s*. The sound was rendered as *hs* under an earlier transcription system.
z	is like the *ds* in 'fa*ds*'
zh	is unaspirated, and sounds like the *j* in '*j*ug'
a	sounds like '*a*h'
e	is pronounced as in '*he*r'
i	is pronounced as in 'sk*i*'(written as *yi* when not preceded by an initial consonant). However, in *ci, chi, ri, shi, zi and zhi*, the sound represented by the *i* final is quite different and is similar to the *ir* in 's*ir*', but without much stressing of the *r* sound
o	sounds like the aw in 'l*aw*'
u	sounds like the *oo* in '*ooz*e'
ü	is pronounced as the German *ü* (written an *yu* when not preceded by an initial consonant) The last two finals are usually written simply as *e* and *u*.

Finals in Combination

When two or more finals are combined, such as in *hao, jiao* and *liu*, each letter retains its sound value as indicated in the list above, but note the following:

ai	is like the *ie* in 't*ie*'
ei	is like the *ay* in 'b*ay*'
ian	is like the *ien* in 'Vi*en*na'
ie	similar to 'ear'
ou	is like the *o* in 'c*o*de'
uai	sounds like 'why'
uan	is like the *uan* in 'ig*uan*a' (except when preceded by *j, q, x and y*; in these cases a *u* following any of these four consonants is in fact *ü* and *uan* is similar to *uen*.) ue is like the ue in 'd*ue*t' ui sounds like the 'way'

Examples

A few Chinese names are shown below with English phonetic spelling beside them:

Beijing	Bay-jing
Cixi	Tshi-shi
Guilin	Gway-lin
Hangzhou	Hahng-jo
Kangxi	Kahn-shi
Qianlong	Chien-lawng
Tiantai	Tien-tie
Xi'an	Shi-ahn

An apostrophe is used to separate syllables in certain compound-character words to preclude confusion. For example, *Changan* (which can be *chang-an* or *chan-gan*) is sometimes written as *Chang'an*.

Tones

A Chinese syllable consists of not only an initial and a final or finals, but also a tone or pitch of the voice when the words are spoken. In *Pinyin* the four basic tones are marked. These marks are almost never shown in printed form except in language text.

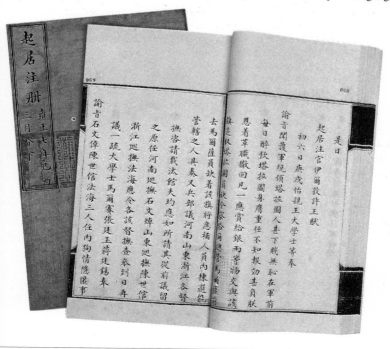

Index

204